LIGHT IN THE LAND OF SHADOWS

Sermons For Advent, Christmas
And Epiphany, Cycle B
First Lesson Texts

Harold C. Warlick, Jr.

CSS Publishing Company, Inc., Lima, Ohio

Library of Congress Cataloging-in-Publication Data

Warlick, Harold C.
    Light in the land of the shadows : sermons for Advent, Christmas, and Epiphany : Cycle B, first lesson texts / Harold C. Warlick, Jr.
        p.   cm.
    ISBN 0-7880-0769-6 (pbk.)
    1. Advent sermons. 2. Christmas sermons. 3. Epiphany season — Sermons. 4. Bible. O.T. — Sermons. 5. Sermons, American. I. Title.
BV4254.5.W37   1996
252'.61—dc20   96-5304
                                                                                                      CIP

This book is available in the following formats, listed by ISBN:
    0-7880-0769-6   Book
    0-7880-0770-X   IBM 3 1/2
    0-7880-0771-8   Mac
    0-7880-0772-6   Sermon Prep

PRINTED IN U.S.A.

Dedicated to Rosemary Keller,
Skin Parker, Eleanor McCall,
and Marjorie Hill, who frequently
lend their seasoned presence
to the University Chapel.

Table Of Contents

Introduction   **7**

Advent 1   **9**
Evergreen Wreath And Faded Leaf
Isaiah 64:1-9

Advent 2   **15**
The Warrior And The Shepherd Are One!
Isaiah 40:1-11

Advent 3   **21**
Lighting A Fire In A Cold Room
Isaiah 6:1-4, 8-11

Advent 4   **27**
The Giver Becomes The Receiver
2 Samuel 7:1-11, 16

Christmas Eve/Day   **33**
Light In The Land Of Shadows
Isaiah 9:2-7

Christmas 1   **39**
All Dressed Up And Somewhere To Go!
Isaiah 61:10—62:3

Christmas 2   **45**
A Little Book Of Comfort
Jeremiah 31:7-14

Epiphany 1   **51**
(Baptism Of The Lord)
Point Of Origin
Genesis 1:1-5

Epiphany 2   59
    Any FAX Or E-Mail From God Today?
    1 Samuel 3:1-10 (11-20)

Epiphany 3   65
    Will We Enjoy Heaven?
    Jonah 3:1-5, 10

Epiphany 4   71
    Religious Load-Management
    Deuteronomy 18:15-20

Epiphany 5   77
    Turning A Minus Into A Plus
    Isaiah 40:21-31

Epiphany 6   85
    A Bad Temperament Can Kill You
    2 Kings 5:1-14

Epiphany 7   91
    When Imagination Replaces Memory
    Isaiah 43:18-25

Epiphany 8   99
    Pain And Promise In The Heart Of God
    Hosea 2:14-20

Transfiguration Of The Lord   105
    Swing Low, Sweet Chariot
    2 Kings 2:1-12

Introduction

Initially, let me thank you, the reader/preacher, for daring to open this book and give some credence to preaching on the First Lesson. When first given the challenge by the publisher to produce sixteen sermons on the Old Testament lessons for Advent, Christmas, and Epiphany, I pursued a common course. I went to three seminary libraries and searched through 23 years of lectionary sermon books from denominations on cycles A, B, and C to see how others had handled the First Lesson. Alas, I discovered that, for the most part, the common denominator seemed to have been: "Avoid it and preach on the Gospel or Epistle lection."

Convinced that a closet Gnosticism is still practiced by many who view the Old Testament as "dead wood" in the face of Christian revelation, I decided to start from scratch. As connections between the Old Testament and the season at hand emerged, I began to reaffirm my belief that the Old Testament presents to us a God of love and the New Testament shows us just how much that God loves us. It is, perhaps, futile to speak of the intensity of God's love without first connecting with the reality of God's loving nature as portrayed in the total historical dimension of the Old Testament. Hence, the absolute necessity of preaching on the First Lesson in this or any season confronts us.

The enclosed sermons are fleshed out in normal, everyday language, grammar, and sentence structure. They are meant to be comprehendible for a wide audience. Yet the faithful preacher can take comfort in the fact that they are backed up by sound biblical exegesis. While the sermons are couched in modern issues, compelling stories, and specialized needs, the goal of each sermon is to enable the congregation to reach an informed understanding of the text and integrate that understanding with daily life.

The sermons are longer than the minimum needed in hopes that enough material will be presented to enable the preacher to refine, rearrange, clip, discard, and reinterpret whole sections without losing the essential message or winding up with too little in the way of resources. However you choose to craft your work, what lies within these pages is now yours. Whatever is helpful, please use. Whatever is trite, please disregard. I'm certain that your efforts will improve these messages and lift them to a standing and effectiveness far higher than this original author could have achieved himself.

Evergreen Wreath
And Faded Leaf

The occasion was a joyous one as the young bride and groom settled into their seats at the head table at the Country Club. Like most wedding rehearsal dinners, the environment was heightened by candles, flowers, special music, expensive clothes, and family and friends who had not seen each other in years. Most likely many would not embrace one another again until the next family wedding or a funeral shivered its way to the forefront. All the proper symbols of hope were present in the room: the greenery, the gifts, the invocation from the preacher, the wedding photograph (touched up as only a professional earning top dollar can effect), and the round of toasts.

As the toasts continued, from the humorous to the meaningful to the absurd, the clanging of utensils on glasses ceased when the mother of the bride rose. She was a graceful woman. She exuded charm, beauty, and class. For forty years she had hung together with her husband through a number of his debilitating illnesses and financial reversals. The road she had traveled had been a rough one. But determined pride, the intervention of Alcoholics Anonymous, sheer will-power, and belief in God had helped her persevere and maintain that marriage. With a glint in her eye and a smile on her lips, she addressed her daughter and future son-in-law. Her toast was as simple as it was profound: "Honey, I hope

9

you and your husband will be as happy as your father and I *thought* we would be forty years ago."

That paradox, the apparent contradiction between hope and despair, expectation and reality, provides a fitting backdrop for this season we call Advent. All the proper symbols are here for the season of hope: the candles, the flowers, the special music, the gathering of the family of God, the exhortation of the preacher, and the expectation of gifts still to come. For four weeks we will focus on the incredible hope that is Advent: God coming to save God's people. For four weeks we will relive that anxious expectation like a young bride or groom: Israel waiting, Mary waiting, John the Baptizer waiting. Yet the paradox is still there. Contrary to our usual manner of celebration, Advent begins on a note of despair, not hope. All the human schemes for self-improvement, eternal bliss, and ethical responsibility by the people of God have taken us to the realization that we cannot save ourselves.

The first lectionary lesson rushes us into the paradox. Advent with its wreath of evergreen, symbol of life, of growth, of hope, is rushed back 2500 years to Isaiah and his recognition that "we all do fade as a leaf." That's the paradox of Advent — the evergreen wreath of hope amid the reality that we indeed do all fade like a leaf. The trust in God that is voiced is apparently counterbalanced by a deep sense of desperation, symbolized by a faded leaf so vulnerable it can be blown away into oblivion.

At the personal level we vacillate between the evergreen wreath and the faded leaf. The famed agnostic Robert G. Ingersoll spoke these somber words at the graveside of his brother:

> ...*every life, no matter if its every hour is rich with love and every moment jeweled with a joy, will at its close, become a tragedy as sad and deep and dark as can be woven of the warp and woof of mystery and death.*[1]

Physically our lives do march toward the faded leaf instead of the evergreen wreath. The human body has its seasons commensurate with spring, summer, autumn, and winter. The advancing years take their toll. The eyes dim, the hearing wanes, the hair grays, and the muscles lose their tone. The body becomes as fading as the leaf which will one day fall from the tree. As the ability to concentrate is lessened and the latter days become less comfortable, perhaps many a senior citizen is tempted to toast the next generation with the words: "We hope you will be as happy as we *thought* we would be forty years ago." And, as long as we view the physical life as moving inexorably toward a grand anticlimax, it matters little whether the leaf falls from the tree in a violent storm or gently floats down from an old forsaken limb.

The faded leaf of despair confronts the evergreen Advent wreath in our social order as well. Twenty centuries after the Christ was born and taught his followers that salvation lay in feeding the hungry, clothing the naked, and visiting the sick, we have the technical capacity to free humankind from the scourge of hunger. No child need go to bed hungry, and no human being's future and capabilities need be stunted by malnutrition. Yet where is the evergreen wreath of Advent hope for the 500 million to one billion people seriously malnourished in our world? Do we thrust our well-filled glass in their direction and with a furrow on our brow exclaim: "We hope you will be as happy as our agricultural analysts thought you would be forty years ago"?

Finally, notice how the evergreen wreath and the faded leaf come together in our religious heritage.

Look at the poor Israelites. They were always finding God and just as quickly losing God. Isaiah's sixty-fourth chapter is an intercessory prayer, asking the question, "Where in the world is God?" Some exiles have returned home to discover their temple in ruins, their property destroyed, and their people a bunch of half-breeds without any faith. The prophet prays, "God, you have hid your face from us." Then he vehemently petitions, "Rend the heavens and come down. Let the mountains quake at your presence. Throw your weight around. Belly up to the bar. Make yourself clearly known. Give us another Exodus. Part the sea again. Break your unbearable silence." In other words, "Make us as happy as we thought we would be forty years ago when we prayed for this exile to end."

Likewise, the New Testament provides ample evidence that people sometimes find God but then lose God again. The lame man at the pool of Bethesda wistfully puts his faith in gimmicks and gadgets. Mary Magdalene thinks she has lost God when she cannot find the body of Jesus. Peter denies his Lord and sits down beside the road in despair, having lost the very thing he has prized most — his close relationship with God. And Judas obviously has God at his elbow for years but loses him, even unknowingly betrays him.

It happens to most of us. We go through periods in life when God appears close at hand, but we also experience periods when God seems very far away in the heavens and so cut off from the earth.

It is at this point of paradox and darkness that Advent becomes an ever-present need in our lives. Just as ancient Israel under Isaiah's guidance hoped that the Exodus-Sinai events in her memory would be reenacted so life could begin again as it began in the days of Moses, so do we focus on the evergreen wreath hoping that our collective memories of the coming of Christ to the world so long ago will be reenacted in our midst so life can begin again for us.

The faded leaf is but one side of the paradox of Advent. To refuse to embrace the dying of the physical, the social, and even the religious, is to ignore the real ministry of the darkness and its rest. Indeed, all our faded leaves of existence and personal darknesses remind us that all the schemes, expectations, and goals we have set — for ourselves, our world, and our religious organizations — have yet to be redeemed. There's more that needs to come. We, too, join the longing of Isaiah, Mary, and John for God to break into our isolation. We place our wreath of hope alongside the darkness of our faded leaves. Perhaps the paradox of Advent becomes ultimately our one great hope. It is an irrational, apocalyptic hope, which informs our waiting. As Frederick Buechner posits, "The darkness hungers still for the great light that has gone out, the crazy dream of holiness coming down out of heaven like a bride (or groom) adorned for us."[2]

For people like us — ever thoughtful, ever reasonable, and ever realistic — the evergreen wreath of Advent, the special music, the candles, the flowers, and the best efforts of the preacher are necessary. Our wedding rehearsal is necessary as we sit in the darkness and hunger for the bride or the groom of life to come to us. All our hopes twisted together make enough hope to live by, hope enough to see beyond the faded leaf and give us the courage to wait for more.

And this waiting is not easy. The Hebrew word for "waiting" has affinity with a word that means "to entrench." The idea of waiting for God is that of digging ourselves in to God. It means going through a period of our lives trying to adjust ourselves to the truth of God which we know. Waiting requires strength. It is an expression of confidence in the one who, despite the faded leaves of human response, will do something new and surprising and startling, just as has been done before.

The evergreen wreath and the faded leaf stand for the paradox of God's involvement with humankind. From the ranks of the poor, the faded, and the disinherited have come God's liberators.

The similarities between our condition and those of the days in which Isaiah's words were spoken are obvious. We still cry for God to rend the heavens and come down. In the period of darkness, Isaiah's people were brought to the point of knowing that they did not know and understanding that they did not understand. The mystery of faded leaves being transformed into evergreen wreaths is symbolic of the power of God transforming darkness into light in human lives. This transformation spans the whole sweep of biblical history. Abraham, the unbeliever, becomes the obedient servant of God. Jacob, who cheats his father out of something that wasn't his, becomes the loving father of Israel. Moses the angry murderer becomes Moses the patient father of a nation. Peter — the cursing, redneck, abrasive fisherman — becomes the tolerant leader of the church.

Perhaps the biggest transformation recorded in the Bible took place in the life of one named Saul. He made a very big move. He changed from a person of hate into a person of love. It was a big change. He got a second chance and he got it in the middle of his life.

A second chance, early or later in life, is not cheap. Saul wandered around stumbling, blind. People had to lead him around. Saul was used to being in control, calling the shots. He had all the credentials, all the degrees, all the certainties and securities. Suddenly he was detached from all that. He became helpless, needy, and small. He became a faded leaf that could have been blown off the tree of responsibility at any minute. All he could do was wait and hope. Contrary to some popular misconceptions, this one called Saul did not immediately begin his ministry and have his name changed to Paul. He was silent from the Scriptures for at least two years. Those two years must have been quite painful as the "faded leaf" of existence was juxtaposed with his newly-found eternal Savior. He felt the bitter disappointment of his family as they saw the young scholar espouse a controversial cause. He experienced the disillusionment of his fellow Jews when he turned his back on a brilliant rabbinical career. He knew the high cost of renouncing his family, childhood faith, and secure position. Certainly Paul, as appraised by those who were on the other side, appeared to be a personal, societal, and religious faded leaf, ready to be blown from the tree of life. All Paul could do was wait and hope in the eternal. But this hope gave him the vision to see beyond the faded leaf and wait for more.

We begin our journey this year with the evergreen wreath and words from Isaiah about a faded leaf. We wait for more. So be it.

---

1. Robert G. Ingersoll as quoted by Edgar DeWitt Jones in *Blundering Into Paradise* (New York: Harper, 1932), p. 53.

2. Frederick Buechner, *The Hungering Dark*.

The Warrior And The Shepherd Are One!

A friend conveys the story of his childhood misconception about finding his vocational way in life. From his earliest remembrance his goal in life was to own a grocery store. The idea surfaced when he made his first lasting friendship, at the age of six, with a child named Larry. Larry's father owned the movie theater in their small hometown. Every Saturday, he and Larry would go to the children's matinee and they would not have to purchase a ticket. Larry's father allowed them to walk right in without paying. Then, in the lobby, Larry's father would open the glass door on the popcorn machine and the children would each reach in and take a free bag of popcorn. The obvious conclusion my friend drew was that if you own something, all you have to do is show up occasionally and take what you want. Since you own it, you don't have to pay for anything. The way is prepared for you. Armed with that logic, it seemed to him that the best thing to own was a grocery store. You could then show up when you wished and take all the candy you wanted off the shelves without ever paying for any of it.

Never did it dawn on him that someone had to work long hours of preparation, cleaning the theater, popping the popcorn, winding the movies, and putting in much unseen labor and personal finances to keep the place going. Likewise, he assumed that the stock appeared on the shelves of a grocery store by magic and the managers just opened and shut the door in between, taking what they wanted off the shelves. This facile notion of property was quickly dispelled in his teenage years when he secured his first part-time job as a stock boy in a large grocery store. After that he began to focus on any career but owning a grocery store. Behind-the-scenes preparation can be an eye-opening experience, as all of us perhaps realize. There are few, if any, free rides out there in life. The powerful owner must also be the gentle and responsible shepherd of his goods.

In this regard, today's text (Isaiah 40:1-11) can be a tricky one to probe. Its mood is one of hopeful anticipation. Israel has apparently accepted her inability to save herself. She has served her sentence in Babylon, and a voice in the wilderness cries that a new way is being prepared for her. Yahweh will flatten the hills and lead all the long-exiled Jews in a glorious homecoming. Yahweh will move at the head of this triumphal procession as a conquering God. Yahweh's silence has ended. This God who seemed to be defeated by the Babylonian gods will march along the way in a show of unrivaled power. The macho God or the supreme feminist has determined that a hoped-for but unexpected release from prison is to be effected. The owner of humankind is ready to open the door and wave through God's special people on a new way that runs from Babylonian exile all the way to Jerusalem. Here is a people being led by one who should resemble an oriental despot returning from silence and exile in regal power.

Yet the rhetoric is quickly reversed. The God who moves at the head of this powerful and joyous procession is as caring and gentle as a shepherd. The Divine Warrior is also the caring shepherd who watches over the vulnerable sheep.

The ethical responsibilities of a shepherd are enormous. Sheep are the most helpless of creatures. A mother sheep will not move over a few feet to allow her bleating lamb to nurse. Often the shepherd must physically lift the lamb and carry it over to its mother to nurse. Sheep are so easily frightened that they will not drink from a flowing stream because of the noise it makes. The caring shepherd must dip from the stream and fill a huge tub with the water. The Psalmist is simply stating a fact in asserting that the shepherd leads his sheep beside still waters. Sheep will only drink from still waters.

What a contrast is presented in the text: a Divine Warrior who leads as a shepherd. Here is a foretaste of what is to come in the Christ experience. *The messianic perspective merges with the suffering servant motif.* Israel's understanding of her journey along the way prepares her to embrace a messiah who serves or a servant who is also the deliverer. The tough, triumphant liberator is one who purposefully humbles himself as a caring, tender shepherd. Since Israel's vocation is to make known her God, the walk on the way for her symbolizes not only a triumphant return but a new understanding of her role in life. She not only has to experience some kind of magnified warrior but prepare herself to respond in kind to the same type of tender care that is shepherding her. Personal regeneration and social concern are fused into one vocation as early as 2500 years ago. She has to walk in the same way in which her God walks. There is a strong ethical meaning in the very process of her redemption. Her tradition of chosenness and redemption is now set in the direction of ethics.

This effort to bring together salvation with ethical responsibility has always been the stumbling block for Christians and the church. Messiahs and shepherds do not appear to mix. The faith versus works argument seems to run throughout the deliverance message of Isaiah.

The crux of our faith is the radical belief in the entrance of God into the human condition through Jesus Christ. How that was accomplished seems to matter less than the fact that it was. In Jesus of Nazareth, the Old Testament concept of the suffering servant is united with the Old Testament concept of the Messiah. The human shepherd and the Divine Warrior are united. The human identification is extremely important. It places an ethical demand on us. Jesus wept as we weep. Jesus lived as we live. We see a tired and weary Jesus Christ sitting beside a well, asking for a drink of water. He is tired and thirsty. We often overlook this factor in our visible attempts to catch a glimpse of Jesus. In television, movies, paintings, in legends and stories about him, and in children's books about the boy Jesus, quite often the divine side is visible and the human side acts as a drapery around the divine core. The human part somehow never seems quite real. But that is not the Christ of Scripture. When he sits beside a well, a tired traveler, asking for a drink of water, he is not pretending. He is not faking the human emotions. He does not masquerade as human to catch the woman off guard. He is as fully human shepherd as he is Divine Warrior. When, in his teachings, he says that those who mourn are to be congratulated because they shall be comforted, he is speaking of a condition he is able to experience. In the garden of Gethsemane, he experiences his loneliest spot in the loneliest of hours. He prays. He is not pretending. He is not running madly around to hire lawyers to represent him at his coming trial. Nor is he looking for an army of angels to defend him with swords and spears. The shepherd is in agony. He is sweating. He is bundling up his guts and laying them in prayer at the feet of God and saying, "Help me!"

If we want to walk on the Way God has prepared through our earthly wilderness, we must prepare to have faith in the Divine Liberator and a resolve to take on his role of shepherd. This demands all the Advent preparation we can muster.

Excerpts from *The Doctrina* show that "the Way" is a term which had come by the end of the first century to have an exclusively ethical meaning. There had been efforts to develop Christianity along nonethical lines into a mystical "spirit" to the neglect of morals. The apostle Paul had to fight off a boastful band of false prophets in Corinth who maintained that the gifts of the spirit delivered one from bondage to an evil world. As such, those who possessed the knowledge of this Divine Warrior need not concern themselves with the fleshly obligations of a shepherd in an evil world. What emerged from this battle with Gnostics, perhaps hardy forerunners of today's New Age proponents, was a clear Christian belief that no amount of knowledge was the Way of the Christ that was not also evident in a person's own way of tenderly caring for the other brothers and sisters on the planet. The hardy antagonist of heretics, the author of First John, struck a blow for ethical Christianity when he wrote: "By this we may be sure that we are in him; he who says he abides in him ought to walk in the same way in which he walked."

What is this Way? Not sentiment but sharing; not benevolence but caring; not a macho or supreme feministic power to liberate alone but a shepherd's tender care that the pain of another is our pain as well.

The words are familiar: "Prepare the way of the Lord; make straight in the wilderness a highway for our God." Behind-the-scenes preparation can, indeed, be an eye-opening experience. "Prepare the way of the Lord." These words bring to us the atmosphere of Advent, of John the Baptist, and of the expectation of the birth of Christ.

Sometimes on figures standing at street corners in big cities, on billboards by the highway, or on posters stuck around sports arenas we can see the placard inscribed: "Prepare to meet thy God." Indeed, but what kind of God? If God is as much tender human shepherd as divine liberator ready to intervene from the outside, then part of our Advent preparation must be arranging to be where that shepherd is most likely to be found. When we feed the hungry, touch and let ourselves be touched by the AIDS victim, clothe the naked, welcome the stranger, assist the homeless, and shepherd the defenseless among us, we soak ourselves again in the thought and language of the Bible. We prepare the Lord's road; we build God's highway through this desert of human exile for so many of our brothers and sisters. We move out of our old highways with their deep valleys and lumpy hills, rough surfaces and dusty corners. And as we fill up our world's valleys and work on its dangerous corners, we not only create great arteries for others, we also prepare the way for the deliverer/shepherd to come into our own hearts. The Warrior and the Shepherd are one. So be it!

Lighting A Fire
In A Cold Room

His name was Father Dominic. He spoke English fluently and he was on a sabbatical leave from his post in France to study in America. He was old beyond his years, a man whose physical resemblance was that of an eighty-year-old instead of his rightful age of 58. At once you knew something was not quite right about him. Father Dominic's teeth ground together when he talked. His eyes were like a monkey's eyes, much too large for the small face that housed them. He appeared to stare right through things and people. Father Dominic sprinted everywhere he went, as if life had left him behind and he was desperately trying to catch up.

One day he explained his insatiable appetite for rushing through time. "I was caught in France as a young man during the World War II German occupation," he began. "One winter I had no wood to light a fire and the cold weather broke my health. The room was dark and so cold, so cold," he chattered. "I contracted tuberculosis and all I could do was shiver in a corner night after night, all winter long. I would have given anything to have had some candles or just one little fire in the fireplace. I needed some fire in that cold room."

How contrasting is that need to light a candle for warmth and illumination with a world whose use of fire has become too often cosmetic. As we approach Christmas, this is a time of candles and fires. We enter a season where fires are lit in even the warmest of rooms. People in sun-belt states will rise Christmas morning and lay a huge fire in their fireplaces. Then, with their air conditioners running full blast, they will sit by the crackling fire and open their presents. The ambiance, not the need, necessitates the fire.

Sometimes the Advent candle means but a furthering of the religious ambiance of the Christmas season. We light the candle for the candle's sake. Yet God never lights a candle, in human hearts or elsewhere, for the candle's sake alone. God lights fires in cold rooms, cold hearts, and cold societies for illumination and warmth. No soul is truly saved until it becomes, in a direct sense, a savior to other souls. The fatal blow to any faith is when it is regarded as an end in itself.

Earl Grey wrote of his father, a former Governor-General of Canada, "He lit so many fires in cold rooms."[1] What a beautiful eulogy to have earned. There are so many cold rooms in life. Some are cold for lack of wood and coal, like Dominic's forced impoverishment. But most are cold for lack of sympathy, meaning, humility, friendship, and hope.

Today we find our inspiration in thinking of a young Isaiah who went into the temple at Jerusalem with a dejected spirit. Fearful problems faced his world and the man who was supposed to deal with them, King Uzziah, had just died. Isaiah's world was like a cold, dark room. In that temple he apparently found a soul-reviving warmth that redirected his whole purpose. Perhaps we can do the same as we examine our own reason for being in a house of worship in our day and time.

Once Dr. Harry Emerson Fosdick gave four wrong reasons why people come to church.[2] There are people who come because they believe it to be the decent thing to do in the normal American community. In other words, they are there to light the candle for the candle's sake.

There are people who come because they are fans of the popular preacher. Just as others admire athletes, movie stars, and entertainers, they admire the preacher. In other words, they are there to light the candle for the candle's sake.

There are those who come because the church helps one's reputation in the eyes of community social respectability. Again, they are there to light the candle for the candle's sake.

Then there are those who think of worship as a glorified Bufferin tablet to guarantee or induce a little peace of mind away from the petty problems of business and family.

Today's text has little interest in those wrong reasons. It is totally saturated with the positive and creative reasons people come to worship. It is a text for those for whom life is lonely, empty, and unfulfilled. It is a text for those who are confused by the noisy clatter of a technological, materialistic world in pursuit of the proper Christmas gift and have come to earnestly ask, "Is there any word coming from the Lord?" It is a text for those who experience moral incompetence, aching fears, and a life whose structures are becoming twisted. It is a text for those who need a soul-reviving warmth and a mind-edifying illumination.

Isaiah's vision happened "in the year that King Uzziah died." That great king had raised the kingdom of Judah to its highest levels of peace and prosperity since the glory days of David and Solomon. The proud young Isaiah must have had great dreams of the future for his nation.

Unfortunately King Uzziah spoiled all that. King Uzziah was a religious man. But he was also a man who loved power. One day, swollen with his importance, he marched into the temple and decided he would be the priest. Taking a golden censer filled with incense, he went into the Holy Place, where only the priest had a right to go. Well, the officiating priest told King Uzziah that wasn't how things were done. Uzziah became red with rage. He never attended worship after that. He sort of retired from religion and kept his son, Jotham, at home. And young Jotham never forgot that. He never formed the habit of worship attendance in his childhood since his father had quit. In his young and tender years, he never sat down and thought the matter through.

The Bible tells the complete story of Uzziah's son, Jotham. He was 25 years old when he came to the throne. Scripture says, "He did what was right in the eyes of the Lord, as his father Uzziah had done, but unlike his father, he never entered the temple of the Lord" (2 Chronicles 27:2).

Jotham had leadership ability and he was smart. He was an excellent businessman. He was energetic and he was a builder. He regarded the temple as an asset — great for the community and its people. Consequently, he donated a large sum of money to it. In fact, he even constructed an upper gate for it. If it had needed a pipe organ or a stained-glass window, Jotham would have mailed in the money for it at the drop of a hat. He was a religious man. He was also young and successful. He was busy organizing armies, building businesses, and shaping the destiny of his city. If you had asked him, he probably would have candidly told you, "Doing good and taking care of my family is my religion. At least I'm not a hypocrite."

Jotham never understood why the people acted corruptly under his leadership and why, ultimately, all the spiritual fruit fell off the vines in his kingdom under his son Ahab and his daughter-in-law, Jezebel.

Yes, Jotham's father, King Uzziah, went to worship, but he quit when the priest and his associates would not let him light the fire, swing the incense, and smoke up the Holy Place for his own ends. That decision, to light the fire for the fire's sake, on the part of Uzziah affected a whole generation, especially his own son.

The call, vision, and response of Isaiah contrasts sharply with the lack of call, lack of vision, and lack of response on the part of Uzziah.

Uzziah, full of self-sufficiency, marched into the temple trying to be his own priest. He was, in his own mind, God's representative on earth. He felt comfortable in his success and holiness.

Isaiah, on the other hand, went to the temple with a feeling of darkness, coldness, and desperate need. He felt uncomfortable with earthquake disturbances deep in his soul.

Uzziah, full of power, demanded to go into the throne room of God and worship for his own sake. He took the golden censer filled with incense to smoke up the Holy Place.

Isaiah, on the other hand, found himself stripped of all human egoism. He looked up and saw himself in the presence of the

King of kings and Lord of lords. In spite of the crumbling of earthly thrones, Isaiah saw God still on God's throne. His pride blanched before the white-hot holiness of God. "Woe is me!" he cried. He saw deep in his soul a self-centeredness that needed to be cleansed. God's smoke filled the entire temple.

Uzziah's response to the barrier placed by the human priests in front of his ego was to fly into a rage against them. This rage was like a live coal which burned hot within him and led him to keep his son, Jotham, at home. Uzziah emerged from the temple with the dread mark of leprosy on his forehead. As he thundered away from the temple, having been refused the chance to light a fire for the fire's sake, he probably retorted, "If you ever need anything, don't send for me." Then, he entered a dark, cold world of the leprosarium for the rest of his days.

By contrast, Isaiah's response to the voice of the Lord saying, "Whom shall I send? And who will go for us?" was quite direct. "Here am I. Send me." And he emerged with the mark of the prophet on his head and a fire in his mouth which could never be put out.

The text points us toward powerful contrasts in the motivations of two men, both of whom considered themselves religious. One tried to light a fire for the fire's sake, and the other found the fire purging him of his coldness, darkness, and despair. The text is a proper one for us this season.

Isaiah had something awakened in him by the setting worship provided. The name of the priest, the songs the choir sang, and the context of the readings were not listed as having been particularly important. What was important was the fact that Isaiah had a place to worship, and a proper motivation within his soul with which to worship.

The church is important for the relationships and settings it provides. Even in this day of automation and mass media, there is still a need for us to worship with our brothers and sisters. Dial-a-Prayer and Dial-a-Sermon are nice conveniences. Yet they are not all we need. Watching a service on television is perhaps better than no service at all. Vending machines would perhaps be more efficient for distribution of the Lord's Supper. Yet in all of these something is missing. The ability to confess deeply requires a relationship with other human beings, sinful people if you will. God makes himself known to sinful persons among sinful people. That is the only means of balancing the budget in one's soul and lighting the fire in our cold rooms so we can see the coming of Christ. So be it!

———————

1. As quoted by W.A. Cameron, *The Potter's Wheel* (Toronto: McClelland & Stewart, 1927), pp. 219-220.

2. See "What Are You Doing in Church," pp. 73-81, in Donald Macleod, *Higher Reaches* (London: Epworth Press, 1971).

The Giver
Becomes The Receiver

The text for today lifts before us Yahweh's choice of the family of David as the vehicle for God's divine gift to humankind. Yet the message marked a transition in David's status. According to the passage, David wanted to build Yahweh a "house." He proposed to do what all self-serving rulers in that ancient world would have done. Much of Israel's worship life was well established at that point. The tent which housed the Ark of the Covenant was a recognized institution. A conviction began to emerge that God dwelt within this tent in its Holy of Holies. King David wanted to build a divine residence of cedar which would contain the Holy of Holies.

Nathan originally blessed this idea. But God changed God's mind and offered a second opinion. The temple would be built by David's son, Solomon. Instead, Yahweh would make David himself the "house" of God by guaranteeing his embodiment concretely in this man's family and dynasty. What a transition. The achiever, the one who wanted to give the gift to God, became the receiver of God's gift. The "Davidic idea" became fixed in the imagination of Israel and is to this day in Advent remembered as initiating the coming Christ.

One of the amazing aspects of the Bible is its honesty. The sordid aspects of human experience are included with the positive aspects. Human failure and human triumph comprise the environment for God's revelation. The guilty and the guiltless find their way into the pages of this chronicle of God's revelation to humankind.

The scriptures use the example of David's desire to do something for God to teach us all a lesson about patience, waiting, and freedom. The changed mind after David's quick conclusion points to a particular character of the God of the Bible. This God is a come-and-go God whose dynamism cannot be settled or confined to one place. Unlike every other god, this God needs no house, wants no house, and has no house. At a deep level the housing project denial points toward David's love for God. Daniel Day Williams is correct: "Love always makes itself vulnerable by willing the freedom of the other."[1]

The love David displayed toward Yahweh and Yahweh's freedom was no small matter for that time and place.

In preliterate and simply-structured societies, religion played a unifying role in life. The village was a self-contained society in which all rituals and symbols were religious ones. "The religious" was not relegated to one aspect or activity of life, distinct from the other aspects. Speaking of the religious and the nonreligious or secular as two different dimensions of life would have been foreign to a preliterate society. To live at all was to live within a religious community with clearly defined rites of passage on the journey home. Every major event in life, from pregnancy and childbirth to the cutting of the first tooth, puberty, the first haircut, marriage, and vocation carried religious rites of passage like clear signposts along one's ultimate journey home.[2]

A wholeness of outlook characterized the civilization of David's time. The private and the social were not separated from one another. Religion tended to unify or support all elements of life, both social and individual. David's recognition that God needed no house was a fundamental aspect of his being allowed the honor of the "Davidic ideal" which ultimately produced the Christ child. Only as David was willing to "let go" of his desire to bring a gift to God and let God bring the gift to him, was the revelation made complete. The text is more than a rhetorical inversion. It is a powerful message for today's Christian. We, too, are called to let go and let God bring God's gift to us.

Do you remember your first day of school? It was one of life's great separations. Perhaps your parent drove up the circular driveway of an elementary school. You perhaps clutched her hand as tightly as possible as you passed legions of strangers on their way to the classroom. You stood at the door and, perhaps, she literally had to push you in. The classroom probably appeared to be the most foreboding room you had ever entered.

Looking back, that time of "letting go" of mother's hand was a necessary step. It was indeed the time to "let go" and enter another experience. Life is essentially a series of separations. We let go of certain experiences in favor of other experiences. Friends are gained and then we are separated. Sometimes couples marry and at other times they separate. Sometimes our "letting go" involves places: we leave our hometowns; we leave our schools; we even leave our churches. Sometimes we let go of roles or patterns of relating. We let go of our roles as parents, as children, as students. Sometimes we even "let go" of attitudes and beliefs. In those moments of "letting go" we come to realize how intensely loyal we are to the people, the places, and the attitudes which have shaped us.

Letting go is a necessary part of life. The Bible is full of separations. Abraham and Lot separated so each could live and multiply. In the newly-found freedom as humans with a mind of their own, Adam and Eve had to separate from the Garden of Eden. In the book of Exodus, God told Israel: "I have separated you from all the people that are on the face of the earth" (33:16). David was told to let go of the idea that he controlled God's housing needs. Jesus himself was separated from his family and his family's business. In order for the early church to be more than four little families meeting together in upper rooms to remember Jesus, those people had to separate and trust God to come among them in God's own freedom.

God has given our human personality many weapons with which to encounter life and find the way home at the end of it. We possess fight and flight responses, administrative ability, anger, ego, temperament, grief reaction, and the like. These characteristics sometimes make it difficult for us to simply let go and wait for God to be God.

The Bible tells us that right after he was baptized, Jesus Christ faced the greatest temptation of his life. He had just realized that he was the Messiah. He was at the point of beginning his ministry. Satan tempted him to try to live his whole life in a moment's time. Satan promised him instant accomplishment of his ministry. Listen to the account: "The devil led him up to a high place and showed him in an instant all the kingdoms of the world. And he said to him, 'I will give you all their authority and splendor ... so if you worship me, it will all be yours' " (Luke 4:5-7). Just like that, promised the devil. Instant achievement. No waiting. No having to grasp the slow wisdom of the world. A shortcut, just for the taking, in an instant, was held forth. But who was deceiving whom? The devil was merely offering to Jesus in a shorter span of time what would ultimately be his anyway. God had promised Jesus that achievement from the very beginning at Bethlehem. The devil was merely offering Jesus something he was already promised. But the devil did offer it to him in an instant. That was the difference.

We moderns often find ourselves unable to let go of our need to be in charge and allow God to bring to us the gifts God wants to give. The late L.D. Johnson used to contend that one of the bizarre facts of life is this one. The more religious people become, the less patient and comfortable they become with the mystery and freedom of God. Those who consider themselves very religious tend to point their finger at us and claim God is this or God is that. The freedom of God is the heart of all religion. You'd think the closer you got to God the more overwhelmed you would be by the awesomeness and indescribable nature of God. You'd think the closer you got to God the less clear-cut would be your expression of God.[3]

David's ability to step back and let God provide him with the same gift he wanted to give God was an impetus of inversion that was reflected in the grand gift to come. No greater ruler ever commanded the Israelite people. David was depicted as God's personal choice to lead the chosen people. He unified the two nations of Israel and Judah. He was impetuous, aggressive, charismatic, manipulative and, above all, a great administrator. He removed the last vestige of Canaanite power in the land.

But when David allowed the inversion to take place, when he allowed God to give him the gift, he established a process which foreshadowed the coming Christ. Kings normally give gifts. They do not receive them, especially from God. Consider the images used by the descendant of David, Jesus the Christ, to provide this same wonderful good news.

Jesus washed with water. Whether it was the smelly feet of the disciples or his own baptism, he showed that this image was definitely a change. He took a towel, wrapped it around himself, and washed the smelly feet of his disciples. That was, indeed, out of sync. Everyone knows that disciples wash their *master's* feet. The proper image is of a religious leader like our society's Pope in Rome sitting on an altar with a huge canopy of gilded bronze ringed in Renaissance splendor by the Swiss Guard in their scarlet and gold. That's image projection at its finest, is it not? Everyone knows that winning coaches have coliseums named after them, author books, do television commercials, and have swimming pools in the shape of their school's mascot. Messianic coaches do not go into the locker room after the game, take out towels and basins of water, and start washing the smelly feet of their players. Yet this crazy son of God would do just that. That's a powerful image, one must admit.

Secondly, Jesus gave suppers with bread and wine to show that his new life was a brotherhood or sisterhood. That, too, is an image that shocks us. Banquets are given in honor of great people; great people do not give banquets for the poor.

Jesus touched people with his hands — whether they were lepers or diseased or dead, like Lazarus. He touched people society would *not* touch. What a reverse image projection that was! Most of the societal projection of a great religious leader is the number of *important* people the leader touches — the winning coach, the Hollywood actor, Miss America, the converted infamous criminal, the bestsellers. Not Jesus! His hands touched those that society would *not* touch.

31

This strange process of inversion which makes us the receiver of a gift from God is the essence of our Advent hope. Advent recognizes a transition in our status as worshippers of God. We are now the receivers of the ultimate gift: God in Christ comes to make us the house of his dwelling. This notification is as heady for us as it once was for this precarious tribal chieftain named David. There is no greater joy that can be promised us.

---

1. Daniel Day Williams, "The Vulnerable and the Invulnerable God," *Union Seminary Quarterly Review,* Vol. 17, No. 3, p. 225.

2. Some of the material in this sermon has been previously published in Harold C. Warlick, Jr., *Homeward Bound* (Lima, Ohio: CSS Publishing Co., 1991) and is used by permission.

3. As quoted in L.D. Johnson, *Moments of Reflection* (Nashville: Broadman Press, 1980), p. 39.

Light In The
Land Of Shadows

On a trip to Munich, Germany, Samuel Miller had a chance to watch Karl Vallentin, the last of the great "metaphysical clowns." As the curtain lifted, the stage was completely dark except for one small circle of light in the middle. Vallentin appeared in his magnificent clown costume and began to intently look all around the circle of light. A policeman appeared on the scene and inquired if he had lost something. The clown replied, "Yes, the key to my house." The policeman joined him in the search for a long time and finally asked, "Are you sure you lost it here?" The clown answered, "No, I lost it over there," and pointed to a dark corner of the stage. "Why, then," asked the exasperated policeman, "are you looking here?" To which the clown shrugged his shoulders, "Because there is no light over there!"

In a very real sense this sometimes depicts our religious situation. We decide where God is to be found and if God comes in another form we are in the position of the clown, of looking for God where God does not exist.

This was true of those people before that first Christmas who expected the Christ to be born in a mighty display of power and positive experience. They looked for him in the temples and their emotions. Few thought that God's lordship would be expressing itself in the dark corners of the world, among the poor and disinherited.

God is not always to be found where the brightest light is shining. Sometimes God's justice is not even center stage, because the shadows of life are not center stage. And it is often in the land of shadows that we find the key to our lives.

The lectionary text for today is an intrusive one. It is closely related to the political ideology of the Davidic monarchy in ancient Israel. A new king is welcomed with all the dazzle surrounding important births and coronations. This celebrative rhetoric announces a new heir who will bring light and newness as the fulfillment of long-standing expectations on the part of people who have lived in the land of political shadows. The message of the great light comes as a welcomed announcement to people who look forward to the dawn of a completely new day for their shadowy world.

The prophet Isaiah has in his mind's eye a people who are suffering in a land of shadows: the fearful military domination of the Assyrian empire. These men and women, who once experienced God's covenant with Moses, are enduring unspeakable brutality at the hands of the Assyrians. They have been thrown politically into the pit of the shadows — sheol, the land of deep darkness in which there is no hope.

The prophet announces a new creation for these dwellers in the land of shadows. Hope is reawakened. And that hope, that floodlight of joy, is not to be found center stage in the decisions of the great powers. The text goes on to point not to the triumph of the new king's military armies but to the power of "justice" and "righteousness." This new king will rule not in self-aggrandizing power but in the best hopes of the old Mosaic covenant. The key will not be found where the world has traditionally found light — in the center-stage brightness of power, success, and prosperity. The people will not have to walk over to the armed light of another political rally as resplendent as Hitler's festival of lights in pre-World War II Munich.

No, the light will itself come into the shadowy places of the world, dispensing justice like a "Wonderful Counselor," an "Everlasting Father," and a "Prince of Peace." Small wonder, then, that the church finds Isaiah's oracle so useful and appropriate for its Christmas announcement of Jesus.

We, too, are dwellers in the land of shadows. We live in a world that desperately cries out for the dawn of a new beginning in the material realm. In the shadows of our existence we lock our doors and chain our bikes at night. We often hide in our churches in the shadows of stained glass windows and collection plates full of dollars, blaming faceless, nameless enemies for a lack of progress. Ours is not a peaceable kingdom. One out of every nine jobs in the United States is related to the Department of Defense. More than half our national budget is related to defending ourselves in a world of war. A kind of spiritual gridlock develops when significant numbers of Christians decide it is easier to blame evil than to make a clear proclamation that the light has come to brighten the dark places. Sometimes this spiritual gridlock develops in our own soul when we try to wander around in the shadows of past experience instead of proclaiming a new birth.

Leslie D. Weatherhead was the venerable pastor of the City Temple in London, England. In a little volume titled *When the Lamp Flickers*, Weatherhead noted that all of us sometimes try to "bury Jesus in past experiences." Many of us perhaps had a wonderful experience of religion years ago. Perhaps we heard a resounding message, or read a book, or walked in solitude under the quiet stars and made an agreement with God. We gave God who and what we are. Our sincerity could not be doubted. The reality of God's presence was known to us and we walked on air for days. Yet the remembrance has become just that, a remembrance. Some call it a testimony, a testifying to what once was. But here again, we cannot treasure that experience or even revive it and live on it forever. Christ is not waving from our personal pasts but is out in front of us, beckoning us to new experiences, new birth, and new spiritual adventures. Christ's government is not through an old, old story but through an "ever-expanding peaceful government that will never end."

The prophecy from Isaiah touches us, then, at both the personal and collective levels as we respond to its claims. While our homes are filled with lighted Christmas trees and toys, we still look for the light to come into our lives. All too often, like Vallentin's clown, we look for the key in the center-stage phenomena of power politics and powerful religious emotions. It's as if the coming dawn of the new realm cannot find its way into our shadows. Yet Isaiah's tying together the announcement of the king with the power of "justice" and "righteousness" firmly foreshadows the Christmas event.

For example, let us contrast the Christian and Buddhist nativity stories. The Buddhist nativity is heroic and embroidered with myth. The Buddha is depicted as being born to a beautiful queen in the "unconquerable" clan of Shakya. He is born to a life of princely luxury and advantage. He enters the womb of Maya in the form of a white elephant, and after 500 previous incarnations comes to this final and glorious birth. As his mother's time comes near, she retires to a pleasure-grove where she is attended by thousands of maids-in-waiting. The garden is full of flowers, fruits, and nuts. While the queen stands beneath the greatest tree in the grove, she gives birth to the infant Buddha without pain or discomfort. The child is delivered in a gold net carried by angels.[1]

The Christmas story is quite different. Instead of an aristocratic and noble birth, we are told the story of a carpenter's wife from a poor village. The birth takes place in a donkey shed. The animals in whose feeding trough the infant is laid are the only witnesses to the birth. There is no golden net held by angels, nor great tree. And this one so lowly born is forced to flee into Egypt to escape Herod's threat of slaughter.

His very birth takes place not on the center stage of world history or in a tremendous personal religious experience, but among those who are forced to sit in deepest darkness.

It is always from the deepest darkness that the light shines brightest. Isaiah's words are spoken first to those who have lived longest in the shadows. He prefaces his announcement by speaking of the humbled land of Zebulun and Naphtali (Isaiah 9:1b).

When the Assyrians come swooping down on Palestine in 722 B.C., the people of Zebulun and Naphtali in the remote regions in the northwest part of Palestine are the first to be brutalized and carried away as captives. Those who remain behind are, by the time of Isaiah, the longest standing mourners in the kingdom. For hundreds of years they have had no reason to hope.

In like manner, Jesus' ministry is exercised first among those who have dwelt longest in the shadows. He does not go first to the great cities of Palestine. It is to the little village of Nazareth, in the area of Zebulun and Naphtali, that Mary and Joseph bring the baby Jesus after their return from Egypt. And it is to this region that Jesus many years later returns to begin his ministry.

It is to these dwellers in the shadows that Isaiah speaks as he announces the shining of the great light and the dawn of the new kingdom. The Christmas event, like the ministry of Jesus, establishes "justice" and "righteousness." That the Christ has the power to bring light into the shadows of Zebulun and Naphtali unleashes the most radical kind of hope for humankind. This light can bring together the different families of the human race with eventual advantages to all. Insofar as humans have relied on this light for deliverance, forgiveness, and guidance, God has confirmed that faith.

A child has been born to us. He has been rightly called the Wonderful Counselor, the Mighty God, the Everlasting Father, and the Prince of Peace. He sits over a kingdom and rules, unlike other rulers, with justice and righteousness from now to eternity.

The Kingdom whose foundations we commemorate and the Prince whose nativity the world's nations celebrate today bring light to all us dwellers in the land of shadows.

---

1. See Conrad Hyers, "The Nativity As Divine Comedy," *The Christian Century* (December 11, 1974), pp. 1168-1172.

All Dressed Up
And Somewhere to Go!

In Tennessee Williams' play *Sweet Bird of Youth*, the heckler says to Miss Lucy, "I believe that the silence of God, the absolute speechlessness of God, is a long, long and awful thing...." The late Carlyle Marney retired from his church in Charlotte and went to Wolf Pen Mountain. There he waited for God to say something. He confessed that he had figured if he could get some time completely free from his preaching, his church work, and his worldly obligations that God would really jabber. After five years of waiting, hiking, hoeing, splitting wood, sleeping, praying and studying, he finally reasoned that God had had ample time. But the inscrutable silence simply pushed him back on resources, memories, and ideals he already had. With great certainty he said, *"It's as if God has said all God intends to say."*[1]

Indeed, sometimes the speechlessness of God can be a long and awful thing. Such silence creates a kind of skepticism in communities about whether God has any coming salvation or not. The historical backdrop for today's text is similar. It helps us understand the wellspring of hope embodied in the promise of Isaiah. God will finally break God's silence, dress God's people, and give them somewhere to go.

Jerusalem had been leveled to the ground in 587 B.C. by the armies of Babylon. Much of the population had been marched off to the Tigris and Euphrates river valley areas. There they had lived in exile for the next fifty to seventy years. Not until the rise of Cyrus of Persia, the Abraham Lincoln of the ancient Middle East, were they freed to return to their homeland.

As the Hebrew people returned to their homeland with great optimism, the mood changed. Life became very bleak. Their optimism was abruptly challenged by tremendous economic difficulties. With few financial resources, meager food supplies, and harsh weather conditions, the people found the task of rebuilding their once proud homeland next to impossible. They had come home to a forsaken and abandoned city in ruins.

God seemed silent. God had made promises and the people had believed in them, but what had been promised had not materialized. God had, indeed, brought them back home. But their new life fell far short of what the exilic prophets had promised. To this disappointment the prophet Isaiah spoke God's word. Israel appeared to be a poorly-dressed people with no place to go, believing in a God who was apparently neglectful, indifferent, and silent.

Israel had nothing to wear, no word from God, and nowhere to go. Other nations had apparently noticed. They concluded that God was both impotent and indifferent.

The scripture, like the season of Christmas, heralds a remarkable transformation. God breaks the silence, dresses the people for the occasion like a bride on her wedding day, and elegantly proclaims a salvation through a most unlikely vehicle. Everything changes. The watching nations see God's awesome sovereignty. Something unexpected, wondrous, and irresistible fires out of history. The God who "loves justice" alters the circumstances of the oppressed and the brokenhearted. There has been no divorce between God and God's people. To the contrary, there has been a grand and glorious wedding. The prophet hammers home the reality with powerful imagery.

When you are going to be wed, it's only proper to expect some special clothes for the occasion. God plays both father of the groom and mother of the bride. Israel is decked out in a tuxedo of salvation and a wedding dress of righteousness. The needed garments are provided. Israel has been turned into a crown of beauty. Her smelly rags and humble surroundings have become the dignity and glory of the whole world. God, the divine tailor, is at work again! A new wellspring of hope is rising from the ruins and remains of defeat.

The divine tailor always weaves a fabric of glory out of the shame of human history. When Adam and Eve are thrown out of the garden of Eden, naked, sinful, and vulnerable, the divine tailor makes garments of skin and clothes them. They can rise unashamedly only in the clothing which God provides. Those clothes are woven by God's goodness. Out of nakedness and dirt, God's salvation and righteousness clothes Adam and Eve in new-birth-every-day attire and gives them somewhere to go. There is no need to hide or to be ashamed.

The divine tailor takes beaten, drab, defeated Israel, coming home to a wasteland at the end of exile, and fashions a wedding dress of salvation and righteousness. From her history comes a marriage that produces a child enabling all to rise unashamedly only in the clothing of righteousness. This new-birth-every-day attire gives them somewhere to go. There is no need to hide or be ashamed.

The divine tailor takes the smelly rags of shepherds and the swaddling clothes of a child in Bethlehem and fashions a wedding dress of salvation and righteousness for humankind. A world naked, vulnerable, and offensive has no need to hide or to be ashamed. Through the unlikely vehicle of a tiny Jewish babe, God's goodness fashions a wedding garment of salvation and righteousness.

The teachings of the divine tailor are clear. From the garden of Eden to the parable of a lost son who returns in rags from a pig sty only to have a father remove the filthy clothing and dress him in fine garments, God covers God's people for the occasions of celebration.

We are, indeed, all dressed up. Yet God's purpose is much larger than a lesson in haberdashery. There are few statements sadder than "all dressed up and nowhere to go."

So we've been clothed. So we've been made beautiful. So the rest of the world can see in our Christmas lights, candles, cantatas, and presents that we have been redeemed. What next? What does it mean to wear the clothes fashioned by God for us?

Just as God breaks the silence of indifference and neglect after he clothes his people, so does he expect his people to break their indifference and their neglect. Isaiah hammers home the message. God redeems not for the sake of Jerusalem alone. The ones clothed in garments woven from God's love are to become the human agents of God's transformation of God's world. God's people are not only all dressed up. *They have somewhere to go.*

God's people are not to stand quietly on the church's walls, dressed in royal garments, and remain silent while friends die of cancer and AIDS and the world tears apart through war and hunger. We are called to break our silence so all may come through the great tragedies in life with a spirit of hope. We are to break the silence and indifference of our privileged positions so others may be able to recover from the pain and suffering of their past events.

Ten years ago an African-American woman called a North Carolina pastor. She told him that she had moved to the state two years earlier from Georgia. Her sole purpose for the move had been her little boy. He played the viola. She enrolled him in the North Carolina School for the Arts and took odd jobs to enable the two of them to survive financially.

His mother explained to the pastor that she had picked church phone numbers out of the yellow pages and had been calling all morning. No church had been able to help her. Her son had never played before a live audience. She wondered if the pastor would help her by letting the boy perform a concert in the church. He had to go to Washington, D.C., the following week and audition for a scholarship. She stated, "We're here with very little besides a dream for him. We moved the whole family and spent all our money for that dream."

The time was hastily arranged for him to play in the church. Around sixty people turned out to create an audience and help the boy in his quest. As the well-dressed citizens sat in the fashionable church on Country Club Drive, the boy and his mother walked in. He was 13 years old. He wore tennis shoes and an old felt jacket, much too short for his arms. He had never owned a suit. He was tall, thin, and awkward looking. His shyness was almost reclusive. But he could play the viola. His talent was something special.

After his concert, one of the men in the church came up to the pastor. He said, "Some of us have been talking. We can't sit here in our nice clothes and let that boy go to an audition in Washington in tennis shoes and a felt jacket. He'll be competing against well-heeled people from elite backgrounds. We must at least dress him."

Several of the people collected a sizeable sum of money and called the mother. Early the next week the mother and son went to a department store and purchased the first two suits and new pair of shoes the boy had owned. A church member later commented to the pastor: "You might as well kiss that money good-bye. You'll never see any return on that. What a waste. Whoever heard of a black viola player, anyway?"

Seven years later the pastor received an envelope in the mail. Enclosed was a newspaper article clipped from the feature section of *The Winston-Salem Journal*. The headline of the half-page article read "Winston-Salem Musician Is Chosen to Play at Carnegie Hall." Underneath the picture of the tuxedo-clad young man was a hand-written sentence: "A dream that has come true."

Christ is born. We stand dressed in God's salvation and righteousness. Christ is born and the party has begun. We've been clothed, protected, and made beautiful. We've been set free and forgiven. We're all dressed up. *But let us never forget that we have somewhere to go.*

---

1. Carlyle Marney, "Our Present Higher God," in *To God Be The Glory,* edited by Theodore Gill (Nashville: Abingdon, 1973), pp. 52-61.

A Little Book
Of Comfort

The lectionary text for today is part of a larger unit that has sometimes been called "The Little Book of Comfort." Old Testament scholars view Jeremiah 30-31 as a collection of independent oracles inserted into the book of Jeremiah to introduce the hopeful chapter 32 where the prophet of doom evidences his faith in the ultimate redemption of God by purchasing a field at Anathoth.[1]

Certainly all of us need our little books of comfort. Life deals us its downs with its ups, its discomforts with its comforts. We practice certain idiosyncrasies of comfort which can be summoned to assist us in situations where despair and anguish seem to be our only options. Many a child will sit in a worship service and make it through particularly boring sermons by counting the number of pipes on the organ or the number of light bulbs in the chandeliers. It provides something to focus on through the perceived difficult ordeal of the moment.

Our society has witnessed a proliferation of "Little Books of Comfort." Many individuals find it helpful to read daily meditations that speak with compassion and offer solace and guidance on such issues as intimacy and relationships. Most widely used are perhaps those which give a measure of support for individuals in a Twelve-Step program. People seeking hope for lasting recovery from sex addiction, alcohol addiction, and other forms of negative addictions would not be caught without their book of daily meditations. That little book of comfort is a day-by-day reminder of their belief in a Higher Power. When we enter many general bookstores today, we find that some books which would formerly have been cataloged as "Religion" are shelved under such headings as "Inspiration," "Spirituality," or "Wellness and Recovery." Little books of comfort serve like a crucifix or rosary in providing people daily wisdom and hope in situations of potential defeat. Today's lectionary text may well have been read as part of a larger "little book of comfort" by the exilic community of Israel. It deserves its place in the shelves of "wellness and recovery."

In a genuine way the second Sunday after Christmas is a time for us to open a little book of comfort as we seek some wellness and recovery. Many of the Christmas gifts have been returned or broken. Family members have returned to their place of residence. The Christmas bills are beginning to arrive in the mail. Perhaps the invitation to Israel in exile, uttered by Jeremiah, can bring us some glad imperatives.

The text responds to a people who live in resignation. It chronicles the possibility of newness. It calls forth a hopeful imagination out of a memory of deadliness. It asserts that the promise of God, sealed in covenant, has been saved. Israel is called to notice something new. A great pilgrimage of people is headed home. These are people who never thought they would have a home. Included in their ranks are the blind, the lame, and the pregnant women. These vulnerable and dependent people are always at risk. After speaking to these pilgrims in the first person, God addresses the nations, putting them on notice as to the coming wellness and recovery of God's vulnerable people. The speech is one that breaks the gridlock of resignation:

1. The other nations can do little to prevent God from faithfully leading his sheep.
2. Creation will be redeemed. Death will be beaten back and reliable "brooks of water" will transform the arid environment.
3. Older people and younger people will engage together in celebrative parties.

4. Priests and people will live together in a restored community, anchored in God's creative joy, life, and gladness.

In short, the people with horrible memories of exile, defeat, desperation, and despair are called to embrace the fact that God will deliver on God's promise/covenant with them. God's outrageous generosity will be on display for the nations to witness. The darkness of exile, despite its best efforts, has not been able to defeat the promise of God.

The people who have believed only in a promise, when there was no tangible evidence to support it, have a new creation. They only have to trust God's generosity.

Christmas itself is an act against the darkness that threatens life. Jesus' ministry reiterates the power of God to push back the darkness of life, and his resurrection attests to the fact that even death cannot overturn God's new creation.

All of us need a little book of comfort as we try to live our lives believing in this promise of new life.

Alfred P. Sloan, Jr., built the General Motors Corporation. His wife, whom he idolized, died and Mr. Sloan was inconsolable. He sat like a granite cliff, strong and rugged. This man who had put together one of the giant industries in our country and possessed one of the most brilliant organizational and scientific minds in history, called a minister friend to his Fifth Avenue apartment. He opened the conversation by saying, "I want to ask you a question. I want a straight answer. I don't want any equivocation. And I want the answer to be yes or no, based on facts. My wife has died. She meant everything to me. What I want you to tell me is this: Will I see her again?"

His friend looked at him and said, "The answer is yes."

All of us want some straight answers about the Promised Land. What's it like there? It's obviously a difficult question to answer without equivocation because none of us has ever been there. Jeremiah lived centuries ago and the connection between our society and his may not offer the same tribute to wellness and recovery.

All we can do is live our lives believing in that same promise of a new creation. The image of a promised land after this earthly life is over is hardly a Christian phenomenon. Some religions have been quite specific about the nature and location of this future home. Geronimo, the great American Indian, wrote of a home in the American West that the god Usen had created for each Apache. The religion of Islam depicts heaven as a marvelous garden filled with wonderful food, drink, and companions. The heavenly home is so graphically described in the Quran and in other Muslim literature that many Muslims are quite eager to die in order to achieve this paradise. Life after death is one of the most ancient and persistent hopes of the human race, yet it is such an uncharted experience that some believe it may be a testimony to the power of wishful thinking.

One of the obvious powers available to us when we believe in a place beyond our earthly time is the power to stand up to the things we fear most. If you have to see something to believe in it, then your life will not accomplish much. A man by the name of William Lloyd Garrison got it into his mind that slavery was against the will of God. Yet everywhere he looked the survival of the economic system depended on slavery. He lived by the promise that an economic system lay in the future that could be prosperous without slavery. He lived by what he could not immediately see.

A woman named Susan B. Anthony lived by a promise. She, in 1857, stood up in a teachers' meeting and introduced a resolution that women should be educated on a parity with men. The mob became so furious she had to slip out a back door. The presiding officer said women getting an education would be a sin and the beginning of the end of marriage. They threw rotten eggs at Susan B. Anthony in Syracuse and waved knives and pistols at her. Finally, in Albany, New York, policemen had to be placed all around the building where she spoke and the mayor sat on the podium with a loaded revolver to protect her. The public argued that if you educate women on an equality with men — listen to this — you'll destroy their biological urges and they will not want to be the mothers of the human race. Susan B. Anthony lived by the promise that women could go to college and still have biological urges. She got that right.

In like manner, Jeremiah's little book of comfort flings a strident speech of God into a society trying to understand its own cultural situation of despair, defeat, and dehumanization — God promises to act against exile. Whenever people live in resignation, believing no newness is possible, God invades the world and overturns exile. God replaces mourning with joy and darkness with light.

Christmas is an act against exile. Jesus' teachings are acts against exile. Jesus' miracles are acts against exile. Jesus' resurrection is an act against exile. And Jesus' promise of heaven is the ultimate promise for us against exile.

The people in Jeremiah's world are told that God is against exile. Israel is invited to believe in that promise and sing along. God saves the promise. The deathly grip of the past is broken.

We, too, are a great pilgrimage of people headed home. We are in a season which proclaims that God has once again invaded the world and created newness of life.

The God who gives us Jesus of Nazareth is a God who keeps a promise.

---

1. See Elizabeth Achtemeier, *Jeremiah* (Atlanta: John Knox Press, 1987), p. 86. This work is part of the *Knox Preaching Guides*, edited by John H. Hayes.

Point Of Origin

The beginning of the world's story is our story. This magisterial word "create" suggests no point of origin other than God. This creation is an absolute new beginning which carries profound implications for what it means to be a human being. For the universe and humankind to be created by God demonstrates the surprising and uncontrollable power of God. For humankind to be created in *the image of God* indicates a uniqueness that leads to a significant purpose in life.

Despite the first five verses of the Bible being among the best known in all of scripture, their significance is often overlooked. The perspective that the universe and human beings are *created* sets the biblical perspective apart from other, competing perspectives in life.

Consider other perspectives of human development which often translate into practical consequences. The way we theorize about our origin and purpose often shapes the way we treat others. If we view human beings solely as highly-developed animals, we can find much to back up our claim. Certainly a biological or anthropological perspective has the weight of research behind it. We humans, indeed, still share 98 percent of our genes with chimps. We are indebted to Homo erectus as our Homo sapien ancestor. Perhaps a magic twist in 0.1 percent of our genes within the past 60,000 years did create the anatomical basis for spoken complex language. Certainly as long ago as Charles Darwin's *The Descent of Man*, it has been pointed out that we are similar to other animals in being subject to the same laws of development from primitive forms in nature, passing on variations by inheritance from individual to individual, reproducing in greater numbers than can survive, and possessing body parts we no longer use such as a tail bone to carry a tail, an appendix to store food when we ate only plants, and wisdom teeth with which to crush bones.[1] If we believe that humankind is solely a part of nature, a species of animal and nothing more, then we are likely to treat the people we encounter as highly-developed animals. Those we like we view as pets. If they love us and remain faithful to us, we cuddle them as we would any friendly and lovable dog or cat. We will bring them into our household circle of friendship and even try to curry the favor of others as we, too, seek to be friendly animals. To those who are unfriendly, we act as if they are a swarm of flies at a picnic or a beast of burden. We ask our school teachers, our police, and our courts to protect us from these pests. We organize our labor force and our economy to enable us to take advantage of these beasts of burden, paying them lower wages and creating social programs to see that they are fed, watered, and sheltered. While all this is quite unconscious, it still reflects an understanding of humankind as animal: pets, pests, and beasts of burden. That is a perspective upheld by many.

Other thinkers view the human being as simply a unique creature that knows it's going to die. If, indeed, we are the only animal that knows it's going to die, what value is love, if we only return to common clay? The existentialist perspective raises genuine questions about the meaninglessness of life. If life ends for us as individuals and eventually for the cosmic scheme, why bother? Why marry? Your spouse is going to die anyway! Why even bother to preach this sermon? All of you are going to die anyway! We are helpless victims. The older we get the more aware we become of the impending end. Consequently, perhaps the best we can hope for is existence today as we eat, drink, and be merry and a painless suicide tomorrow when self-consciousness and good health begin to wane. The human being as a helpless victim of life's forces is a perspective upheld by many.

Finally, consider the perspective that the human being is more like a machine, a complicated but efficient machine. This perspective animates education and industry. In a computer age we tend to view people as data. This perspective doesn't pay much attention to "feelings" as long as the machine produces the goods. As long as the machine functions well it gets rewarded with merit raises and job security in the business world and good grades in the educational institution. We don't hand out bonuses or *cum laude* honors based on "feelings." When the machine becomes older or weaker and falls behind in production or starts making poor grades, we try to repair it. Retraining efforts, continuing education courses, tutoring centers, counseling agencies, and quotas abound. We even have affirmative action programs to make certain every machine gets its chance to perform or be repaired. When the machine stops going altogether and stops performing, we get rid of it, flunk it out of the institution, or dispose of it in some suitable way in a retirement center on the edge of town. That the human being is a machine is a perspective upheld by many.

The first chapter of Genesis is an irreplaceable portion of scripture because it gives us an analysis of the human predicament. It maintains that the universe and the humans within it were *created* by God. It upholds the goodness of this creation and proclaims a vision that all human beings, the ones we see on the street and ones we never see, whether in hospitals or prisons, are something like God. If we hadn't heard this scripture so many times and thought about it so little, we would see how blasphemous it sounds against other practical perspectives of life.

The lectionary text is more than God bringing order out of a surging chaos. It is more than the wind (*ruah*) which gives life and restrains the waters. It is more than the voice of a ruler on a throne who speaks in a sovereign voice. It is more than a God who calls into existence things that do not exist. It is a new beginning, a new perspective which continues to be blasphemous. *God created!* The order and the goodness presented in the first five verses moves symmetrically toward a grand climax. The order in the universe finds its climax in the freedom bestowed on human life.

The good priests in Babylon who compiled the account with striking resemblances to the Babylonian story of creation, the *Enuma elish*, moved beyond the details of Babylonian order to view humans not as slaves or machines, not as unique creatures, not as animals, but as very "images of God." Genesis 1 defines an element of goodness and freedom. The "images of God" are called upon to exercise dominion and care and finish off the creation.

That is the *biblical* perspective: the human is a created co-creator. The human is no pet, no pest, no beast of burden, no machine, no victim. The human being is a co-creator in a created universe.

The human self is holy. It lives in dialogue with its world, its creator, its fellow humans.[2] It shares in creation. It has the freedom to create its own history. Among all the animals it is most helpless and unfinished at birth. It creates things from the materials of its universe, from the words you read to the paper on which it is printed. It creates time through memory and imagination. And it co-creates itself. It overcomes handicaps and blows great opportunities. For seven or eight hours each night it dies through sleep and must rise the next morning to create again.

Each night you and I die. And each morning you and I rise from the dead to create, almost literally. We exist, to be certain, but as for the world we live in, our family and friends, the work we are committed to — we are dead for a while. Then, without even a hallelujah chorus, we wake up in the morning.

Each day we all enact the familiar biblical metaphor of death and creation, of sleeping and waking. Each year we all enact the metaphor of creation, of standing at bay the chaos of past experience and bringing to birth a new historical recognition. January is the time when we mark a new beginning, a new creation, on our calendar-conscious minds.

Both the calendar and the Genesis 1 text call us to reflect on this strange Christian term, "epiphany." The word means "to make known." Essentially, it's when something is recognized for what it is. When the wise men saw Jesus and knew what he looked like, that was an epiphany. Actually, Jesus was not the Messiah or the Savior until somebody recognized him as the Messiah. Like in sleep, it's perfectly possible to be unaware of what's going on around you. Each year Epiphany is celebrated on January 6. It's the time after Christ's birth when people recognize him not as the babe in a manger, but as the Lamb of God. Only when people recognize Jesus as the One who can take away the sin and despair of the world does Christmas mean anything.

A student made his first *A* in a course in graduate school. The school was on a British-type system. It had a reading period in January for two weeks and then students took exams. After the exams, everyone took off for home or snow skiing or warmer climates. When students turned in an exam, they gave the professor a stamped, self-addressed postcard. The professor would mail the grade. The day before this student was to leave for home, he received the postcard in his dormitory mailbox. It said *A*. He was an *A* student. Well, actually he wasn't quite. You see, all the others had departed on their trips. As the dormitory proctor, he had to stay there and lock up. There wasn't anyone for him to show his postcard. He was not recognized yet. All he was was a guy from South Carolina standing in the middle of a dormitory in Massachusetts with a postcard in his hand. Consequently, he caught a bus to Arlington, Massachusetts, where he was on the staff of the Park Avenue Church. He went into Park Florist and showed the card to the owner. "Wonderful," the owner exclaimed, as he showed the card to his daughters. Then he pulled in to visit the owner of the funeral home. And finally, when a friend came in to the local bank to handle the now mangled card, he was really an *A* student. After the hugs, he felt for the first time like an *A* student. It doesn't matter what you are if other people don't recognize you for it.

This is a good time for Epiphany — for recognition. January is when we put away our Christmas decorations. A few more days and the darkness of winter will replace the bright candles which glistened brightly in our windows. It is now that the recognition of the light that shone in Bethlehem must take place. It is now that we behold the promises of the future, of new beginnings.

It is now that we must recognize who we are and what we are about as human beings. It is now that "God created" beckons us into an awareness of what we could become through Jesus Christ.

In 1931, the National Broadcasting Company invited the great musician and conductor Arturo Toscanini to conduct a concert tour of Latin America. The orchestra for the tour was made up of select professional musicians from around the United States.

The group came together on a hot and humid afternoon for their first rehearsal. They began rehearsing Beethoven's Sixth Symphony in a rehearsal hall that was not air-conditioned. These professional musicians had played the piece so many times that they could almost play it from memory. They knew exactly when to come in and when to rest. Usually during rehearsals they could get up and go out for a smoke or a soft drink and still be back in their places in time to play their parts.

If you've ever been to initial rehearsals for a Broadway play, a movie, a musical, or a great symphony, it's somewhat disappointing to be backstage. A card game is going on in one corner. The lead actor is in a room watching the New York Mets. People come running up the steps with a sandwich in hand, throw it in the trash at full gallop, and walk in on cue to give a dramatic performance in their sweatshirt and bluejeans. These people are pros. They can lay down their cards in a gin rummy game and rush out and play a torrid love scene. They can turn it on and off in an instant. That's why they are called professionals.

But something happened that day when Toscanini began to direct. Everyone could sense it. By the end of the first movement no one was daydreaming. Each person was intent on the music. They played it flawlessly. At the end of the final movement the maestro put down his baton. The members of the orchestra rose to their feet in applause. Toscanini stood there until they ceased. Then he said, "That was not Toscanini. That was Beethoven. You just never heard him before."[3]

Perhaps you and I are so familiar with the style and characters of the Genesis 1 account of creation that we can almost recite it from memory. Perhaps these first five verses of the Bible have been subject to more minute examination than any other opening verse of any book, religious or secular. But just maybe a recognition will take place in our lives this year. "In the beginning God created...."

The chapter which follows those words is not a scientific attempt to answer questions as to how life got going. The chapter is not a repudiation of the sexist passages in the other Genesis creation story of Adam and Eve which some have used to demean women. The chapter is not even just a radical break with myths in other world religions which put all the real action with the gods and goddesses. No, the chapter is a statement which governs how we relate to one another today. It is a theological statement about what it means to be a human being.

"In the beginning God created ... it was good." Those are not the words of this preacher. They are not the words of the priests in Babylon who compiled them. That's Word from God. And perhaps we need to recognize that we just never heard God before in those words. So be it!

---

1. James Rachels, *Created From Animals: The Moral Implications of Darwinism* (Oxford: Oxford University Press, 1990).

2. See Reinhold Niebuhr, *The Self and The Dramas of History* (New York: Charles Scribners Sons, 1955), especially pp. 3-5.

3. Thanks to Charles Carter, Forest Hills Presbyterian Church, High Point, North Carolina, for calling my attention to this story told by James Harnish in an article, "What Will You Do With King Jesus?"

Any FAX, Or E-Mail
From God Today?

You and I live in a world of communication. Analysts tell us that most of us will spend two years of our lives on the telephone. Most likely they will not be the best two years. Future generations could spend more than five years of their lives "talking" with people around the globe as they come home from work or school, download their computers, and get out on the information highway.

Calling a college student has changed dramatically in the past decade. Over two-thirds of American college students now have answering machines with recorded messages. According to more than one Dean of Student Affairs, "A telephone answering machine is almost standard equipment for today's college student." In the future, conversation possibilities will be expanded for them by E-Mail and Internet. Even today parents in the United States "talk" two or three times a week by computer to their sons and daughters who are studying abroad.

Certainly our way of conducting business in this country has changed dramatically. Most monthly office telephone bills have over fifty long-distance calls of less than twenty seconds each to answering machines, a host of FAX transactions, and time spent interfacing with colleagues half a world away.

Ah, the age of the communication. We of all people can ask, "Why doesn't God talk anymore?"

As we study background material for a series of epiphanies of Jesus as Messiah, the Old Testament story of God's call to Samuel is thrust before us. Jewish tradition says that Samuel was only twelve years old when he heard God's call to him in the night. This, of course, is the same age at which Jesus dialogued with the priests in the temple in Jerusalem. The stories of the birth, call, and childhood of Samuel could well have been in the mind of Luke as he began compiling his gospel.

Obviously this text has been selected for reading in the Season of Epiphany to illustrate the symbolic correspondence between Samuel's call and response and those of Jesus. Both are "called" as prophets to their own people to indicate the wave of God's future. Both Jesus and Samuel have terrible messages in their hands: God will overthrow the old order of reality because of the greedy and disobedient nature of the religious establishment. Samuel and Jesus are linked by their appropriate response of total obedience to God's "voice." Consequently, to only focus on 1 Samuel 3:1-10 leaves us with but a story of an innocent twelve-year-old being called into God's service. The full text (verses 11-20) is needed to portray the reversal of affairs in Israel that takes place when God's prophet is obedient to God's call.[1]

As you and I sit here on the eve of the twenty-first century, struggling to be obedient servants of God, the lectionary text perhaps throws a dilemma before us. Why doesn't God call us in this time of abundant and easy communication? God called Moses through a burning bush. God placed a call to Abraham through three wandering strangers. God phoned Samuel late at night. God placed a call to Jacob down a long ladder. God whispered to Elijah on Mount Horeb. It would be comparatively easy for God to place a call or give an interview to our world. The tele-evangelists claim to reach the whole world via the airways and cable television. If Jesus came "in the fullness of time," what about now? Wouldn't everyone pause and lend an ear if God used the telephone, the Internet, or a satellite just once and called earth?

In Tennessee Williams' play *Sweet Bird of Youth*, the heckler says to Miss Lucy, "I believe that the silence of God, the absolute speechlessness of God, is a long, long and awful thing...." The late Carlyle Marney retired from Myers Park Baptist Church in Charlotte and went to Wolf Pen Mountain, waiting for God to say something. He confessed that he had figured if he could get some time completely free from his preaching, his church work, and his worldly obligations that God would really jabber. After five years of waiting, hiking, hoeing, splitting wood, sleeping, praying and studying, he finally reasoned that God had had ample time. But the inscrutable silence simply pushed him back on resources, memories and ideals he already had. With great certainty he said, "*It's as if God had said all he intended to say.*"[2] Are there no more direct epiphanies or do we, unlike Samuel, who had a once in a lifetime experience or call, have epiphany overload today?

A key to unraveling the dilemma of God's apparent silence in a world saturated with communication devices is to be found in linking the Old Testament story of Samuel with an assertion in the letter to the Hebrews.

The writer of Hebrews makes a claim: "When in former times God spoke to our forefathers, he spoke in fragmentary and varied fashion through the prophets. But in this, the final age, God has spoken to us in the son" (1:1-2).

The biblical writer insists that God speaks, that God does talk. It begins in the angel's visit to Mary. In plain language the angel says, "Mary, God has been using various instruments to try to communicate to the world, but they haven't been working too well. God has been speaking to all these prophets for generations. But as many times as he has tried to reveal himself, humans haven't listened too well. Sometimes people barked, 'Who's this?' Other times whole societies hung up on him. Then again, some shrewd manipulators put God on hold and proceeded to speak for God. So, Mary, you are highly favored, because God has decided to hang up the telephone, cease these fragmentary and varied little conversations, and open up and tell it all. No more phone calls. No more recorded messages. God is going to make a personal visit and God needs some transportation, a vehicle to get here, or all those humans will hang up on God or say they're out to lunch again. God's going to really jabber this time. He's coming and you are going to be the person to help God get the message across."[3]

A child was born. God opened up and wrote an autobiography in the life of God's son.

Consider the sequence. God had previously talked to us only in fragments and in varied fashion through these people named Abraham, Moses, Jacob, Elijah, Samuel, and all the rest. It wasn't clear enough. Too much static on the line. So God said, "I'm going to come down there and open up and bare it all." And God did. But as God revealed God's self the message led to the cross. Those people who stayed with this child of God and heard him speak went through an emotional roller coaster. They saw him confront the religious establishment, raise people from the dead, and love people as none had before. Then it all turned to despair. Bethlehem's child, the hope of the world, was crudely crucified. They fled the scene in disgust and desolation. Then when they were on the bottom with their emotions, he came back and started speaking again. Their emotions went right back to the top. They were singing and laughing and applauding. One writer said they stayed in the church singing praises to God *for three days.* Then Jesus talked about leaving and God's being silent again. *He told them that if he were to stay and keep talking they would be limited, but if he departed they would be expanded in their gospel.*

What on earth does that mean? Wouldn't we truly be better off with Jesus around talking or at least placing a few person-to-person telephone calls?

James Stuart of Edinburgh used to say that Jesus had to leave in the Great Ascent in order that our religion would be spiritualized. Apparently Jesus wanted a religion that would be a matter of experience and not of appearance or language.

Here, then, is our epiphany. We are called through the life of God in Christ. The Word became flesh. Consequently, instead of responding to a voice, you and I respond to a *life.* A true response to that life of Christ still leads to reversals in nations. A true response to that life of Christ still overthrows old orders of greed and disobedience. You and I have a terrible message in our hands: God's future delegitimizes the entire symbol system on which we have relied every bit as much as it deflated the entire symbol system on which Israel had relied in the days of innocent young Samuel and the venerable priest Eli.

The economics of equality so prevalent in the life of Jesus are a "voice" against the economics of affluence. The politics of justice are a "voice" against the politics of oppression. A sovereign God of tolerance and love is a "voice" against intolerance and hate. God has spoken once and for all. We who have ears to hear, need to hear. That never-ending message shivers its way from first century Israel to twentieth century America. It still seeks receptive ears and hearts to recognize it as a messianic word to a world in trouble. So be it.

---

1. For exegetical background and additional preaching themes, see Walter Brueggeman, Charles B. Cousar, Beverly R. Garenta, and James D. Newsome, *Texts for Preaching: A Lectionary Commentary Based on the NRSV — Year B* (Louisville: Westminster/John Knox Press, 1993), pp. 105-107, and Fred B. Craddock, John H. Hayes, and Carl R. Holladay, *Preaching the New Common Lectionary* (Nashville: Abingdon Press, 1984), pp. 108-109.

2. Carlyle Marney, "Our Present Higher God," in *To God Be The Glory*, edited by Theodore Gill (Nashville: Abingdon, 1973), pp. 52-61. This illustration is also used for the Christmas 1 lesson, "All Dressed Up And Somewhere To Go," p. 39, earlier in the current book.

3. Portions of this material appear in the chapter "No Calls" in Harold C. Warlick, Jr., *Living With Limits* (Lima, Ohio: CSS Publishing Company, 1996).

Will We
Enjoy Heaven?

Many characters in the Bible prove identifiable in our contemporary world. As we sit here today on the downhill side of winter and contemplate the meaning of our lives, one biblical character especially leaps out at us: the prophet Jonah. Most of us associate Jonah with being swallowed by a legendary whale or giant fish. The book of Jonah, however, is actually a poignant parable about the relation of Israel to other nations. The book skillfully and forcefully calls Israel back to her universal mission of preaching the wideness and totality of God's mercy and forgiveness to *all* nations.

In Jonah's day the Ninevites were enemies of the Jewish people. One day God called Jonah to rise and go to Nineveh for the purpose of preaching to them so they could be saved. Full of disillusionment and hatred, Jonah ran in the opposite direction. According to the legend, he told God that the people of Nineveh were not worth saving. Attempting to flee God by ship, Jonah was thrown overboard and engulfed by a giant fish. He resided in the belly of the fish for three days and three nights. In his utter distress he prayed to God constantly but God did not seem to hear him. Finally Jonah was delivered from the belly of the fish. Immediately he journeyed to Nineveh to preach repentance. Alas! the Ninevites repented and God chose to save them. This angered Jonah. He felt that God was turning soft. Embracing his past hatred, he cried out for punishment of the "wicked" people.

The crux of the book of Jonah is to be found in the fact that Jonah emerged from the belly of the fish with the same hatreds and limited perceptions which had accompanied him when he began the confinement. In short, he failed to emerge from a trying situation as a new person.

Fortunately, Christianity is a religion which deals with the sordid aspects of life. Christianity is something to be done. It is a task to be completed, a way of living life on earth. Christianity makes the absurd claim that individuals can live as peaceful men and women in a hate-filled world. It is a peaceful religion. Adolph Hitler, according to his chief architect, Albert Speer, often lamented that Germany had the wrong religion. Christianity's not being a religion of the sword diametrically opposed the Nazi dictator's purposes.

Christianity makes the all-encompassing claim that life on earth has a religious purpose. This planet of ours races through the universe at a fantastic rate of speed. It is a transient planet in an exploding universe. Many people take this to mean that life is utterly meaningless, coming from nowhere and going nowhere. They suggest that there is no purpose behind anything that happens in life. They embody Macbeth's haunting description: "full of sound and fury signifying nothing."

If, indeed, Christianity has an all-encompassing purpose, then our eternal future is with all God's children, as diverse as they are in matters of philosophy, religion, race, morals, and earthly status.

Our American electoral process is the culmination of a tremendous experiment in government. A truly diverse people of all nationalities, income levels, philosophical beliefs, races, and religious persuasions yell at each other for months; then tens of millions vote for one candidate and tens of millions for another. Then, they are all governed by the winners, and the losers subscribe to it. After four years the process repeats itself and the winners hope they have maintained enough positive thrust and programs to enable them to win again, while the losers hope they have changed enough, or conditions have changed enough, to enable them to become the winners. It is a truly blessed way to keep all these diverse groups and people united and working together. It is a miracle we should treasure.

But suppose all those different nationalities, philosophies, races, and religious persuasions had to come together and stay together — forever! When we are thrust together in some urban complex such as O'Hare Airport in Chicago or Kennedy Airport in New York what is most impressive about the horde of people is their differences. It causes us to pause and ask the question, "Will we enjoy heaven?" If God forgives all the rogues and sinners, will we enjoy living with them? If God is that soft, perhaps there is more of Jonah in us than we realize.

Someone once said when he heard of the death of Matthew Arnold, "Poor Matthew, he won't like God."[1] That, of course, was certainly unfair, but it does describe the often critical attitude of Matthew Arnold. It is a legitimate question: "Will we enjoy heaven?"

It is no small question. A man came up to his pastor and asked, "When I die and go to heaven, will I know my wife and children and will they know me?" The pastor shrugged his shoulders and responded, "Why?" He exclaimed, "Well, I think I can make it until death! But beyond that I don't know."

Will we enjoy heaven? Jesus appears to have forgiven everybody of everything — from the soldiers who put him to death to the woman caught in the very act of adultery. He healed Jews, Gentiles, and lepers and even told a common, crucified criminal that he, too, could come into paradise. One can see from our scriptures that Jesus was light years ahead of his time in moving beyond the small walls of prejudice and prohibition.

One of the most profound realities in human existence is the fact that we are all equal down at the foot of the cross. The equality before God of all humans has been a hard pill for humans, especially religious human beings, to swallow. The Lord had said to Jeremiah, "Go into the streets of Jerusalem because Jerusalem is in trouble. But if you can find one truthful person, just one there, I will spare the whole city." Jeremiah did not go. He said, "Lord, the street people of Jerusalem are poor, and because they are poor, they don't have any sense; they are therefore not truthful."

Then there was Jonah. He ran away from God. He said, "I've been running because you told me to go to Nineveh and preach. But, if I did, those weirdos would repent and you are such a soft-hearted God you would forgive and redeem all of them. I didn't go because I want Nineveh to go to hell."

Jonah could embrace God's anger when it was directed against his enemies. But the tenderness of God, especially in the potential repentance of the hated Ninevites, was too much to bear. Jonah was not content to let God be God.

Jonah preferred God to be unchanging and predictable. In this regard, Jonah stands as a warning to the modern church. We must never build our vision of God too tiny to prepare people for living in the mansions of heaven where all the forgiven strangers will come from east and west and sit with us.

Fortunately, even for us, God is not flat and predictable. Our religious response from God is not always nailed down and unchanging. We are not one-dimensional people. Consequently, sometimes we can even be foreigners to our own previous religious perception.

Terminal illness can move us from universal concern into the room of Jesus loves *me* and the Lord is *my* shepherd for a while. Family problems and middle-age crises can move a change-the-world activist into the room concerned with family discipline for a period. Good health and even a college education or personal reading and insight can move a self-centered religious enthusiast into concern for the community and its societal victims for a long period of time. We are called to live, to grow, to move around. Jesus is "Lord of the living," not the dead. The saddest thing in the world is to see a group, a church, or even an individual tear down his or her religious house and construct a one-room, one dimensional dwelling, call it a church and insist that if it is to be a church everyone must live in that one room. This greatly restricts the wideness of God's mercy.

God essentially wanted Jonah to engage in God's process of judgment, repentance, and forgiveness. God came to Jonah twice. God comes to every church and every Christian twice. Our initial attraction usually comes when we grasp the idea of the sovereignty of God. God is, indeed, judge of God's creation. Yet God's nature is also one of tenderness and forgiveness. Consequently God's call is to grow, to be enriched by all God's creation, and learn from it. In short, God has made us and our churches co-creators in that process of judgment, repentance, and forgiveness. God is growing and we grow with God and God grows with us. This process so directly laid out for Jonah is a common denominator which is a recognizable line throughout the scriptures and church history.

Jacob returns to embrace Esau who wanted to kill him. Joseph embraces the very brothers who had sold him into slavery, accepts their forgiveness by God, and states, "I am not judge over you." Mary and Joseph take the child Jesus and flee to Egypt from Herod. They find safety in the very nation and among the people condemned to judgment by Yahweh as the waters destroyed the war wagons of Pharaoh. Barnabas takes Saul by the hand, gives him the ministry to the Gentiles at Antioch, and introduces to the disciples the forgiven former persecutor of the Christians. Jeremiah moves from judgment into hope as he purchases land in the very place he had condemned.

The interesting thing about examining all of church history is that at some point the process must unfold, regardless of the time interval, whereby judgment must tenderly acknowledge and live in the repentance of the other. Consequently if God is alive in our generation we may be certain that God will bring back to us the same message and task assigned to Jonah.

We can take heart in the story of Jonah, for in the end God is as forgiving of Jonah as God is of those in Nineveh. In like manner, when Jesus prays to God that his will be done on earth as it is in heaven, then speaks of forgiving others, he is painting a picture of heaven as a forgiving place. And in his post-resurrection appearances he comes back to those he has forgiven and even breaks bread and is recognized not as a ghost but as one who shares the common meal with as yet imperfect humans. Apparently forgiveness still goes on in heaven when we bring our limited perceptions and judgments there.

Frankly, that should be a great load off our minds. Will we enjoy heaven? Most assuredly. Armed with that certainty, let us

move forward with joy and forgiveness in this wonderfully large
and diverse world. So be it!

---

1. As quoted by Halford E. Luccock, *More Preaching Values in the Epistles of
   Paul* (New York: Harper, 1961), p. 192.

Religious
Load-Management

One of the major ingredients in any kind of endeavor is load-management. A college student, for example, must have special permission from the dean to take more than a certain number of courses per semester. Past wisdom has taught that students experience inevitable time-management problems and personal stress when they overload a schedule.

In the realm of everyday consumption of energy, most cities now have load-management regulators which are placed on homes. City energy departments give a discount to customers who employ such devices. During peak load periods the load-management device will not allow your air conditioner or hot water heater to kick on. This enables the whole city system to avoid going to pieces when the desires and urges of all its customers might overload that system in extreme weather conditions.

For years a certain city had labored with a major soft-drink company to secure an electronic scoreboard for its little league baseball park. Finally the scoreboard arrived and a crew from the city installed it. It worked fine for two games, showing runs, hits, errors, the inning, and the balls, strikes, and outs. Then, rather mysteriously, during the second evening of operation, it froze. The control would not activate it. The lights stayed on the same inning and the same score. It had to be shut down. Someone took the

71

control box home and tested all the connections. They were fine. Consequently, they thought they had big trouble inside the unit. But the next day an electrician from the city came out and it only took him a second, without even looking at anything, to discern the problem: "Somebody pushed all the buttons at the same time," he said. "You can't push but one button at a time." Inside that complicated apparatus is a little fuse. Pump more current into that little fuse than it can bear and it goes out.

The human machine has a little fuse between the ears. It's called a brain. It can handle joy, frustration, grief, love, anger, and just about everything that passes through it — that is, one at a time. Push all the buttons at once and it freezes; it becomes catatonic. Its fuse blows. Even though all the vital signs look great, the big machine shuts down. We call it "being depressed."[1]

Indeed, as conflicts between desires and ambitions, powerful human urges and the prohibitions of society, and dreams and abilities tend to unhinge us and make us "go to pieces," some kind of predictability is needed. Load management is no less real and necessary in the field of religion. There are so many manifestations of God out there to choose from.

Is God a dominant, powerful force ready to lash out at the slightest provocation or shattering of a commandment? Or is God a submissive entity, at the beck and call of every devout prayer group? Is God an exhibitionist or a perfectionist? If most of our human problems have finding a religious outlook on life as a common last resort, is there any consistency which helps us manage the load of competing claims about God?

As a confused and desperate world looks for truth amid many pagan and secular claims, what manages its religious load? Does God have a certain predictable character? The central thrust of today's passage (Deuteronomy 18: 15-20) is a big "yes." In a world of competing religious claims and much human confusion, the Israelites are told that God will raise up a "prophet" to reveal God's will. This "prophet" will be like Moses so everyone will be able to recognize him. This "prophet" will bear remarkable consistencies with Moses.

Jesus' own understanding was in line with the life of Moses. Regardless of the "unhinged" nature of life on earth as it became scatterbrained and went to pieces, God's dealings with humans would be dependable and reliable. There would be no knee-jerk reflexes to human actions, no multiple selves of God responding to various human attitudes. There would be a unified character of God, a certain recognizable predictability, that would manage the load. The key would be Moses' life. It would help ferret out true from false prophets. The old tradition (Moses) would help make the new tradition (Jesus) recognizable. God's revelation would be a continuous and recognizable epiphany.

The parallels between Moses and Jesus are rather obvious. Moses and Israel are in bondage to Egypt just as humankind today stands in bondage to sin and death. The Egyptian pharaoh receives a sign in the form of a dream, consults with his staff, and decides to massacre male Hebrew children. In like manner King Herod receives a sign in the form of a star, consults with his priests, and decides to massacre all male Hebrew children. The infant Moses is rescued from the Nile and secures an Egyptian education. Mary and Joseph rescue the infant by fleeing to Egypt where their son receives his formative training.

The Egyptian soldiers die in the sea by water to give liberation to those who were in bondage. In like manner the waters of baptism symbolize the death of one's old life and the birth of a new one. Moses and Israel wander for forty years in the wilderness where God feeds God's people on manna and at Sinai delivers to them the purpose of their calling. In like manner, Christ is tempted in the wilderness forty days where his purpose is revealed, enabling him to emerge as the bread of life.

The parallels could continue. Suffice it to say that the Exodus and the Cross are tied together with remarkable clarity. Whereas the old exodus delivers a nation, the new exodus delivers a world, a species, a universe. This God who relates to us does so in rather familiar and consistent patterns. Both the Exodus under Moses and the cross of Jesus are actual events in human history, both create groups — the nation Israel and the Christian church — and both proclaim a saving message. This saving message points to the humanness of the endeavor. The Exodus and the Cross are not isolated events, participated in by the generation among whom they occurred. Rather, each generation as it tells those stories encounters the same God at work and experiences the same liberation from bondage to sin and death.

In short, the recognition of the birth of our Savior has to be brought down to earth. It is not a remnant of a fairy tale first learned in childhood, as we encountered Snow White and Sleeping Beauty, or today, the Lion King and Forrest Gump. It is a real, predictable human story. It relies on the most ancient words heard about a Promised One: "The Lord will raise up from you a prophet like me from among you, from your brethren." When he comes, he does not come in the mystery of some other-worldness; he comes as a consistent, down-to-earth, liberating human reality that is recognizable.

Consequently, we find ourselves back there with the Israelites at the foot of Mount Sinai, remembering the clouds and the storm that churned over the heights. We encounter a God who paints in this-world colors and shades so we can manage the competing claims about God in our world. The presence of God is not a psychedelic dream world of legends and fantasy and make-believe. It is the world where rough people bless and curse, where exhausted fugitives from the blessings of society feel real pain, and where people are troubled and preoccupied. It is a very real liberation from some very real problems.

Look at Moses! Look at Jesus! They had to overcome personal torments, inner struggles, self-doubts, and fear through commitment to their higher calling. In spite of their strained and burdened lives, they were so poised and at peace.

The long connection between Moses and Jesus rests solidly on a conviction that God operates not by fate, reflex, or blind chances, but by one predictable, righteous will.

Following the death of Moses the title of prophet served Israel well. When the Christian faith moved into the Greek world, the title was replaced by "Lord." Our joy in the Christ experience has deep roots. Its unity between testaments exhibits a powerful concentration of purpose and drive. Like a river, the unity of God from Moses to Jesus to us, consists not in its absence of cross-currents but in its total flow and main direction.

The tie between Moses and Jesus represents a marvelously integrated God. If ever there was a need to have some clarity in our religious world to manage an overloaded system, such a time is now. Deep within us the messianic passion still burns. People in all lands cry out like ancient Israel for world deliverance. And our overloaded human hopes seem always to betray us. We pant for military messiahs and put our confidence in law, political reform, and social programs. And they frequently fail us as we try to push all the external buttons at once.

And, frankly, the same desperate passion burns in us as we flip the channels of the television, panting for spiritual messiahs on the airwaves. We encounter absorbing devotions — money, prestige, fame — to the pursuit of which all electronic power seems to be subjugated. It's enough to blow a fuse at a low ethical level.

What a load manager is the tie between Moses and Jesus. Authentic religion is always rooted in redemption. Exodus and Cross are symbols of a new aliveness in our own experience. They serve as part of a predictable, continuing force, which keeps on happening to people who find new birth out of the darkness of bondage and death. Even we Christians have to manage our load! So be it.

---

1. This illustration can be found in Harold C. Warlick, Jr., *Homeward Bound* (Lima, Ohio: CSS Publishing Company, 1991), p. 64.

Turning A Minus
Into A Plus

One of the finest minds in our country belongs to a man named Charles Merrill. Charles' father founded a company called Merrill, Lynch, Pierce, a rather successful stock brokerage firm. With part of that vast wealth, Charles Merrill founded the Commonwealth School in Boston. The Commonwealth School has enjoyed a tremendous academic reputation. It has excelled in educating students from diverse backgrounds. On a cold, windy day Charles Merrill and a minister friend were walking to lunch, and he told the minister the secret of his success. He said, "I have a rule in my school that every grade must have at least one teacher who was himself or herself a *C* student in high school. How can someone who has only made *A*'s and *B*'s identify with, educate, and appreciate someone who has to struggle to make a *C*?" He continued, "It is a dangerous half-truth to believe that we are made great by our superior attributes and ruined by our struggles. All of us have minuses somewhere in life."

We should never forget that wisdom. To be certain, we rightly spend most of our lives trying to avoid or at least downplay our minuses. This is impossible to do because all of us possess some weaknesses. Some of these are obvious, like physical impediments — too short, too tall, too overweight, too weak. Others are less obvious — quick temper, shyness, irritable reactions, severe loneliness, insecurity. All our seas are not smooth seas.

The apostle Paul recognized this. As a wise, old, seasoned veteran of life's battles, Paul wrote a letter to a young man named Timothy. He described life in these terms: "It is a fight, and I have fought a good one. It is a hard race to run and still keep your faith. But I have managed to finish that race and still keep my faith. Hence, there is a crown of righteousness waiting for me."

Throughout the Bible, in the lives of so many people, there is the assumption that we can take whatever minuses we have, shoulder them, and with God's help carry them to the very end. The entire Bible chronicles the lives of rather ordinary people who emptied themselves before God and, with God as the center of life, turned their minuses into pluses.

There is a power in this universe that can be a tremendous ally to us. Most of the time we are not aware of it or take it for granted. This power from God is so strong that it can enable us to triumph in spite of our personal and societal weariness.

Certainly ours is a society that can understand weariness, fatigue, and weakness. It's not physical fatigue which lurks as our biggest enemy. To the contrary, we get tired and weak when the conditions surrounding us wear us out. It makes us weary when we contemplate that our foreparents labored for generations for freedom, and we see that racism still exists. Hate crimes still take place. Discrimination remains with us. Young people are still full of despair because joblessness is still here and they can't see a place waiting for them when they finish school. Quite often we tend to embellish our suffering condition and become more weary because we lose contact with our human history.[1] We feel cut off and separated. We can't pull back from life and reflect on the power of God. Our dreams become deferred through our failure to recognize the capacity of God to help us turn a minus into a plus. To regain a wholesome view of life we have to connect with where the rubber meets the road in our day-to-day existence.

Consider this. Virtually everything we've touched today is a living example of a minus having been turned into a plus. We woke up and turned on a light bulb. The light bulb was perfected by a deaf man. Next we might have turned on a radio to listen to the news or some music. The radio was invented by a hunchback.

If we listened to contemporary music we might have realized that three of the eight most popular artists are blind. If we grabbed a quick bite to eat in a fast-food place or in a supermarket we most likely enjoyed a symphony written by a classical composer who was stone deaf at the time he wrote it. Finally, if we rushed to class or the library to continue this grand pursuit called education, few of us acknowledged that the greatest achievement in higher education was made by a woman born unable to see, unable to hear, and unable to speak.

Virtually everything we touch today was invented or sustained by someone who turned a minus into a plus.

The evidence is before us. Our God is a mighty God. Our world has possibilities. Our faith in God can really make a difference in our lives. How can we reclaim that remarkable understanding?

A keen insight into God's power is this lectionary passage from the book of Isaiah. At the time of its composition the Jewish people were in exile in Babylon. They were forced to live far from their native land. They were a weak people in the midst of one of the most powerful dynasties on earth. Isaiah boldly proclaimed: "Those who hope in the Lord will renew their strength. They will soar on wings like eagles; they will run and not grow tired; they will stand and not faint" (Isaiah 40:31).

Most of us, at first glance, would think that Isaiah has the passage all turned around in his ascending order: first you soar, then you run, and finally you are able to stand and not faint! What is this? The developmental scheme seems all screwed up. Don't we first walk, then run, then finally soar like an eagle? That's normally how we turn a minus into a plus.[2] Isn't it?

Isaiah knew God and he knew life. He set down the promises of God in the correct order, for the greatest power and the greatest gift is to keep going when life has slowed us to a walk and we're almost ready to cave in and quit.

God's help is described in three forms. There is the promise that God's help can take the form of ecstasy, enabling us to mount up and soar like eagles. Many times we have felt such joy and celebration in our religious experience. Jesus felt it at the moment when he rode the donkey into Jerusalem as the crowds shouted "Hosanna to the Son of David!" Paul felt it when the scales fell from his eyes and once again when he set foot on European soil. And the women felt it when they gazed into the empty tomb. Sometimes God turns minuses into pluses in a dramatic fashion. It can happen very quickly.

Certainly a quick fix is both a divine and human possibility. A student can receive a *C-* on a paper and as a record in a teacher's grade book. After a particularly urgent appeal for mercy, the teacher can, with the mere stroke of a pen, put a quick vertical mark through the minus, changing it into a plus. The student goes soaring off, flying out half a letter grade to the good. Now, we know that doesn't happen very often. Minuses aren't that quickly eliminated. God is not solely the one who comes barging into our lives with a ballpoint pen, altering the transcript of experience with a quick vertical mark. Sometimes God does — but apparently not very often.

So, Isaiah describes a second way God helps us turn minuses into pluses: "They shall run and not be weary." God gives us strength for activism. God gives us the inspiration to act, to reach out and do a task or solve a problem. We can witness the indefatigable spirit of Jesus as he healed, touched, and spoke to countless thousands of people. All of us have prayed to God and found the motivation and power to get busy with life. We've overcome loneliness through finding purpose in terms of new friends, a club or sorority to belong to; we've found the strength to study harder, to write longer and better papers; we've discovered the commitment to get up and go to church, walk in CROP walks, build Habitat for Humanity homes, and stand for justice. We've found the motivation to run an extra lap, jump a little higher, and pound a little harder. Thank God for the power to run and not be weary, to institute effective church programs and activities.

But, Isaiah is right. There's more power available to us than soaring and running. There are some problems, some deficiencies, some minuses that cannot be attacked by force or energy. Sometimes we can't soar and we can't run.

But fortunately there is another way in which God can help us turn a minus into a plus. "They shall walk and not faint." Now when we seek the spectacular that may not sound like much. Who wants to walk, to barely creep along inch by inch, barely above the threshold of existence, not fainting? That doesn't sound like much of a religious experience, does it? But, friends, most of our decisions in life are made when there is no occasion to soar and no place to run, and when all we can do is trudge along and hear that help is available. When there is a power that enables us to walk and not faint, that is, indeed, good news. It ministers to our greatest difficulty: being able to endure, to be patient, and not to give way to heading in another direction. From the flight to Egypt as a baby, to his night in Gethsemane, to his trial before Herod, to his march with the cross to his crucifixion, the greatest power available to Jesus was the power to hang in there, to walk and not faint, to cling to his situation and not abandon his task.

John Mortimer was an English barrister. He became a great writer. His autobiography possessed a catchy title. He called it *Clinging to the Wreckage.* He asked a yachtsman if sailing the ocean was dangerous. The man replied that it was not if you never learn to swim. He explained: "When you're in a spot of trouble, if you can swim you try to strike out for the shore. You invariably drown. As I can't swim, I cling to the wreckage and they send a helicopter out for me. That's my tip, if you ever find yourself in trouble, cling to the wreckage."

That is one of the most crucial lessons in life: the ability to learn how to start with what you have and build from that, instead of abandoning what you have and swimming for the beautiful shores of already-established activity and superficial soaring. Every existence has its small share of special feelings and bonding moments. Sometimes they seem very remote. But they form a more solid trajectory for the future than the non-experiences of the already-established silver platter. If we've never learned to "walk and not faint," we have never developed resourcefulness and leadership. A sailor who has never sailed in rough seas is never a true sailor.

A Harvard faculty member was asked to address a high school honors class about the secret of his academic success. Surprisingly, he told them his greatest achievement by far was his ability to make a *D* in French each semester of his freshman year in college. That's the accomplishment of which he was proudest. He prayed a great deal that year about his educational efforts. Some of his prayers were naive and some were quite reasoned and sincere. A few were, perhaps, arrogant.

He soared in history with an *A*. He ran through freshman English with a *B*, but in foreign languages he almost fainted. That was his real weakness. He had failed French in high school. He was in way over his head with students more adept in language skills. His roommate dropped the course, and later just dropped out of school completely. Inch by inch this man crept along. And he passed. He hung in there. The teacher even wrote "congratulations" on his final exam, which was also a *D*. That French teacher became his best friend as a teacher. Twenty-six years later as he stood before those honor students, the professor remarked that half the best friends he had on the face of this earth had also been in that French class. What if he had quit?

Some years ago, an American had a series of unique opportunities. In one six-month span he spent an evening with the new secretary of state of Belgium, spent eight days with the United States permanent ambassador to NATO in the embassy residence in Brussels, ate supper with the Supreme Commander of all NATO armed forces, and entertained the Cultural Minister of the People's Republic of China during his first trip to the United States. To each of these knowledgeable people he posed a question: "What do you perceive to be the most prevalent weakness in this generation of Americans?"

To his surprise, each person in various forms pointed to the same thing. The perceived weakness was an inability to tough things out, to hang in there and produce when everything isn't handed to us immediately on a silver platter. The American pioneer spirit of making a plus out of a minus, holding on to the fight, seems to have given way to impulsive grabbing of that which already exists. In other words, it is a loss of the ability to call on the power of God which enables us to walk and not faint.[3]

Let us soar when we can. Let us run, and work, and play. Let us thank God for our great activism. May God always give us the ability to run and not be weary. But above all, let us, "Hang in there. Walk and not faint." Our God is a mighty God. There's a power available to us that can sustain us. So be it!

---

1. J. Alfred Smith, *Basic Bible Sermons on Christian Stewardship* (Nashville: Broadman Press, 1992), p. 99.

2. I'm grateful to John Claypool, *Tracks of a Fellow Struggler* (Waco: Word, 1974), p. 56, for recognition of the proper sequence inherent in the Isaiah passage.

3. This illustration and portions of the sermon may be found in Harold C. Warlick, Jr., *The Rarest Of These Is Hope* (Lima, Ohio: CSS Publishing Company, 1985), pp. 93-97.

A Bad Temperament
Can Kill You

Imagine, if you will, two children walking down a hallway at school. Neither one of them is paying close attention to what he is doing. Consequently, they bump into each other. One child pushes the other down and makes a fist. "He bumped me. He bumped me," the child screams. He is ready to fight.

The other child is headed toward class, realizes there is a class to attend and that the hallway is plenty big enough for both of them to pass. So he wants to go around and continue on his way. The first child is still screaming, "He hit me," and wanting to fight.

Now, we commonly think of the first child as ill-tempered, hyperactive, and incorrigible. Consequently, we are tempted to believe that the difference between the two children is that one is a bad child and the other a good child. Actually, the problem or the difference, most likely, is that the first child has an attention deficiency and the second child does not. His attention can only focus on the moment and it stays there: "He hurt me. He bumped me." The attention is deficient. It cannot see beyond the moment. In a way, it's egotistical. But it is certainly a deficiency in attention. Adults even have attention deficiencies. The person who is angry most of the time doesn't have to be a child. "He hit me. She bumped me. I suffered." You perhaps know a person who reacts instead of responds to an event or a situation. You *react* to a sudden discomfort but you *respond* to life as you focus your attention on something beyond the discomfort of the present. You realize you've got places to go and that the world is large enough for you to walk around that discomfort.

Amazingly enough, Jesus Christ used as an illustration in his very first sermon a man who possessed an attention deficiency disorder and was healed of an incurable disease because he overcame it. Jesus stood in his home synagogue and said, "Many lepers were in Israel in the time of Elisha the prophet; and none of them was cleansed, except Naaman the Syrian" (Luke 4:27). Today's lectionary text from 2 Kings provided the background for Jesus' sermon.

Apparently there was something in Naaman's life that had universal appeal. Perhaps he was similar to many of us. Naaman was a person who wanted healing on his own terms. He could not focus his attention on matters greater than his own life. He was a man of the highest social position. Everyone held him in greatest esteem. Naaman was a victorious general. Life seemed to have poured all its treasures into his arms. Naaman only had two faults: he was afflicted by leprosy, an incurable disease, and he had a bad temper, always wanting life to be on his own terms. Naaman's home was not a very happy place despite his good showing in public. Those two faults, being a leper and an egotist, are not small faults. Naaman's wife must have cried a lot and his children probably did, too. If wealth and luxury lived in that place, so did suffering and fear.

One day a little slave girl told Naaman of a prophet in Samaria named Elisha who perhaps could cure leprosy. "Oh, he's never cured anybody," she asserted. "But nobody has asked him, either. I think he could do it for you."

At that point, the king got involved. Naaman was too valuable a soldier to lose if there was even a thousand-in-one chance someone could save him. "Go, Naaman, go," said the king.

So Naaman did what any of us would do. He made travel plans and set off with as much money as he could cram into his travel bags, about $125,000 in today's currency, to pay for the exotic treatment. He knew that physicians, treatment, and religious healers cost a lot of money. But they are worth it, he thought.

Naaman finally arrived at the prophet's house. What happened then threw him into a complete rage. He was mad because the prophet did not visit with him. Naaman was an important man. But Elisha sent some nameless servant out of the house to tell him to dip in the Jordan seven times. Even today fund-raisers and most preachers know that the wealthy like to be visited personally. Elisha didn't do that. And Naaman grew madder than a wet hen. He was insulted. His attention deficiency rose to the surface. "He didn't visit me. He sent a nobody out to see me." Then, to add insult to injury, the prophet did not heal Naaman the way he imagined a prophet ought to heal people. Naaman had an attention deficiency relative to the manner in which he could be healed. Surely the prophet would call on God, touch the disease, and it would be quickly over. That is what preachers do, don't they? Well, Naaman really got hot then. This dipping seven times in a river was humiliating. He had to do all the work. Finally, the crowning insult was to be commanded to dip in the river Jordan. "If it's only a matter of dipping in a river, why did I have to get up and travel way over here?" I can dip in beautiful rivers in my own land. Why do I have to dip in this muddy little Jordan?" In today's idiom, he would say, "Man, I can stay home and watch better stuff than this on television!"

In a rage, Naaman turned to leave. He decided that he would not surrender his heart. If he could not have healing on his own terms then he would not have it at all. Better to go home and rot and still have your pride than to be humiliated and get well. Now that's a real deficiency in one's attention, isn't it? Naaman's bad temperament almost killed him. "The guy is a fake!" he replied. "He made me angry. I'm mad at the prophet. I'm mad at the church. I'm mad at God. I'd rather go home and rot! He bruised my ego. And insulted me. Better to be a non-insulted leper than a humiliated well person."

Fortunately for Naaman, his servants saw his attention deficiency. They came near to the ranting, raving general and said, "Sir, if the prophet had demanded something great and exciting, you would have done it in order to be healed. Suppose the prophet had demanded $125,000? You were prepared to give it. If he had asked you to crawl back home on your hands and knees you would have done it."

The good sense of Naaman reasserted itself and he began to focus his attention on the big picture. He went down to the Jordan. Can't you just see and hear him dipping himself a few times: "Embarrassing. Boring. This is humiliating. Crummy, little, muddy river. I'm just as leprous as I ever was."

"Keep going. Keep dipping," yelled the servants. Finally he came up the seventh time after he had taken the final plunge. He looked and his flesh was as smooth as the flesh of a little child. It's a great story of healing, isn't it?

We can resonate with that story. Many times in life, we prefer to be a non-insulted leper, in our own way, than a humiliated well person. Sometimes our own attention deficiencies get in the way of our love for life. We want to stay and fight, put up the defense, instead of moving on to the rest of life and walking around the bumps and bruises that have come our way in a world that has plenty of room in which to do just that.

Look at the biblical narrative that way. Consider the little slave girl who first told Naaman about Elisha. She was a war casualty. The Syrians had swooped down on her helpless nation. She had been carried away into a strange land. In one fell swoop she had lost her mother and father, her home, and all of her possessions. She had even lost her freedom. You can't lose much more than that. Then she discovered that the man who was to blame for all that was deathly ill. In all honesty, place us in that situation and most would say, "Let him suffer. I'm glad for every pain his body feels. I'm glad he is getting paid back. He hurt me; now let *him* get hurt. It's God way of paying him back. He bruised me."

Fortunately, her attention was not limited to finding pain for pain, evil for evil. She had been robbed of everything in the way of outward possessions. But there were some values, thank God, that force and violence could not touch. She still possessed a vision of God and love for neighbor that made life worth living. She had something even Naaman did not have. She tried to help a person that she had every right to hate.

Lord, that is so rare to find — so hard to do. But she knew that a bad temperament can kill you worse than leprosy. Each day of life we can see women who have been *wronged* by men, lying in wait for some suffering to beset those who have wronged them. We see men who have been wronged by women, hoping that they suffer, hoping that they get paid back. We can see children who have been wronged by their parents actually glad of every pain of body that the parent experiences. Meet hate with hate. Let evil be returned for evil. What a way to live. They've hurt us, and one day we're going to be there when the house comes falling down. Let's hope our attention, like hers, can be focused on something beyond "he hit me," or "she bumped me," or "I suffered." It is a tough decision, deciding whether to be a non-humiliated and proud sick person or a humiliated, surrendered well person. Maybe we could take the plunge once but not seven times.

Finally, consider old Naaman. Ever been in his shoes? So many have. Life never ceases to amaze us. Suppose the doctor pointed his finger at you and said: "You are terminally ill with cancer. We can see it in your body. You are going to die very soon. But if you will crawl out of here to your car and come back Tuesday with $125,000 for us, we'll cure you." Well, most of us would crawl out of there and somehow beg, borrow, or steal the money. We'd even do that for our spouse or children. You know we would.

Well, Jesus is right on one score. We *are* all terminally ill. We are all dying. Not a single person here is going to get out of life alive. Not one. But there is a cure. Jesus said, "I am God's son. I know where you can be cured. I can't visit all of you, all the time, but you know where my house is. Come down there as often as you can, on the one day a week set aside for that. It is where the treasure is. There may even be some people there that you don't like. But dip yourself into my word and into my values. You have to dip yourself more than four or five times to even notice a change. I don't want all your money. You give what you want to. It's that simple. It is not spectacular. But you will find the cure there to your terminal illness. *You can be saved*."

Sometimes our attention deficiency gets in the way of seeing a greater vision of life. We are important people. We've got important things to do. If all we have to do is dip into a Sunday School lesson, some prayers and hymns, listen to a choir, be with other people in a small building, and listen to a preacher preach from the Bible for eighteen minutes, we can stay home and do better stuff than that. Why do we have to come over here? Better to be a proud, well-slept, enjoyable leper than a surrendered, faithful, and humbled well-person. You know, a bad temperament can be fatal.[1]

---

1. This sermon, for the most part, was previously published in Harold C. Warlick, Jr., *From Cynicism To Optimism, Old Testament Messages For Today's Christian* (Lima, Ohio: Fairway Press, 1990).

When Imagination
Replaces Memory

One of the fascinating aspects of being human is our ability to create time. We have memories and can literally sit in the present but remember and live in the past. On the other hand, we also have imaginations and can literally live in the future. We can sit here and imagine what we're going to do as soon as worship is over.

Most of our problems in life don't come from our imaginations. They come from our memories. The past presents us with a paradox. On the one hand, a lot of good things have happened to us. These things, if remembered, can give us great confidence in ourselves each day. Unfortunately we sometimes forget things we should remember. On the other hand, some bad things have happened to us. We can remember some things we should forget and let them become a lead weight, dragging us into despair. The prophet Isaiah confronts this two-edged sword.

It is a fact that we humans are what we are due to the way we edit our memories. We tend to be selective in terms of what we bring forward from our past.

You know how selective memory works. There are students who can memorize and bring forward the exact batting averages to the third decimal point of the entire starting lineup of the Philadelphia Phillies but can't remember Monday's history lecture.

And some people, perhaps even in our audience, can remember their social club's entire creed and the names of all the members, but can't remember the two names of Abraham's sons.

Sometimes entire nations engage in selective memories. Consider the American Revolution. Our national consciousness remembers the determined colonial settler being pitted against the foreign forces of the King of England. Actually Americans fought Americans. Benjamin Franklin stopped speaking to his Tory son. Only a third of the colonists actively supported the war, and we are told by the historians that nearly as many Americans fought *for* Britain as fought *against* Britain.[1]

And consider our wonderful memories of Christopher Columbus. When he arrived in the New World he frequently hanged thirteen Indians at a time in honor of the twelve apostles and Jesus. Every male over fourteen years of age had to bring a quota of gold every three months to the conquistadors. Those who could not pay this had their hands cut off "as a lesson." Half the 250,000 Indians on Haiti had been murdered or mutilated or had committed suicide within the first two years following Columbus' discovery of the New World.[2]

Remember and forget. Much of who we are as people and as nations revolves around how we edit our memories. Psychologists assure us that the seeds of so many difficulties we experience in adult life were sown in childhood. Many of our fears, inhibitions, phobias, or what not, come to us out of early childhood experiences which we have not forgotten. We leave our childhood behind and come to young adulthood but those ghosts from the past can pursue us. We can leave young adulthood behind and the ghosts from our college experiences can pursue us right into our graves.

This is no small matter. How timeless are the truths we find in the Bible about human life. There is an amazing event in the account of the Israelites' flight from Egypt. At one point the Angel of God, which went before the Israelites as a cloud, had to go stand behind them to help them close the door on their past. At that juncture it was not so much the threat of the Red Sea in front of the people that created the panic as it was the hosts of Egypt behind them. Harold Cooke Phillips is quite correct: "*Is it not true that often our greatest enemies are not those in front of us but those behind us?*"[3] Many of us worry about the job market, the future of our ever-warming planet, and the future threats, from AIDS to cancer. But is it not true that at our base level we, like the Israelites, are harassed not so much by the enemies we must one day meet as by the Egyptians we have already met? This is what makes life so difficult. We have these ghosts pursuing us. We think we have escaped, then we hear the clatter of their horses and see the dust of their chariots! These things harass us because we leave the doors of our memory partly open to them. At some point we must set the Lord our God not only before us but behind us — between us and those memories from the past.

One of Epiphany's wonders is God's capacity to break up old patterns of reality and permit us to begin anew. The lectionary text from Isaiah serves as a pivotal point in Israel's understanding of her mission. She is called to make a sharp break between her past and her future. Her circumstances are to be transformed. Her death to her past will become her very future as she replaces her memories of suffering and abuse with an awareness of God's generous new future.

In this respect Jesus' words have some healing power. "Love your enemies! Bless those who persecute you. Turn the other cheek. If someone asks you to carry his pack one mile, you carry it two miles." Forgive people, how much, seventy times seven? Why this absurdity? "Parents, don't provoke your children to anger." What is this nonsense? Why?

We close the door, my friends. We make ourselves fit for our future. The parents of the Jivaro tribe of Indians in Ecuador have an amazing custom. Every night, when their children go to bed, they linger by their bedsides. They whisper into the ears of the children the names of all the people they must hate when they are older. This is the tribal way of keeping its feuds alive from generation to generation.

The adults can keep their hatred and negativity alive in the minds of their children. Like an acid in the soul, the constant remembrance of evil can eat away at each generation. Such selected memory is a horrible thing.

It creates a lack of emotional confidence in life for each succeeding generation. Very precious things are ruined by keeping old grudges, resentments, and vexations in mind. There are some things we have to forget. If we remember all the hurt we have experienced, life becomes clogged and choked. Life is essentially a process of managing our memories. We should constantly sort out our memories, throwing away things we ought to forget and keeping things that are precious. We either manage our memories or they manage us.

This is easy to say and hard to realize. It is not human nature to forget our unpleasant experiences and remember the good. In fact, Ford Motor Company once conducted a survey among its customers. Ford discovered that the person who has had a positive experience with the car he purchases tells an average of two other persons about that good experience. But the customer who has purchased a lemon of an automobile or had a bad experience with the service department tells an average of thirteen other persons. That's the way we humans are: we remember the ugliness and forget the beauty; we hold to the hate and let go of the love; we remember the cruelty rather than the kindness.

One of the amazing tendencies in life is the ability of evil in the world to shake our faith in God. We all worry about the problem of evil. We study Death and Dying and the Theodicy issue, which, simply put, means if God is all powerful, all knowing, and all loving, why do good things happen to bad people and bad things to good people?

But isn't the presence of good just as big an issue? If there is no God, how do we explain the good? Where did it come from? Isn't the problem of good as big an issue as the problem of evil? How do we account for the beauty of Beethoven, the compassion of Martin Luther King, or the courage of Joan of Arc? Was Jesus merely an accidental collection of atoms?

We should be careful what we remember. There are painful failures in life. There are ghosts from our past that come charging into our present. There are doors that we have to struggle to keep shut. But that is not all of life. In each of us there are some happy memories of times when fortune, even if only for a little while, turned in our favor. Those memories are there to give us joy and confidence, almost like secret helpers, if we do not let the ghosts crowd them out.

Memories are in our lives to strengthen us. And the greatest strength and peace we can know is to get in touch with our childhood knowledge of love. This will take some managing. *Some of us need to recast the memories we have of relationships with our father or mother into adult terms.* Some of us have been moving through life feeling unblessed. We go through life, even if those parents are long ago dead, forever seeking mother's approval or father's approval. Memories gallop into the present from the past.

One of the greatest powers in life is to have our God move behind us and protect us from those crippling memories. And all of us have them. It is a truly adult and Christian experience to recast our past and maybe see now that a father's love was there but was overshadowed by a misguided life or the demands of survival.

In like manner, how wonderful to realize a mother's love was there but was overshadowed by a misguided life or by the demands of survival. Instead of forever seeking our father's approval or our mother's approval, we may have to put God back there and find the ways in which our parents were truly imperfect and truly human like us. Making peace, whether face-to-face or in the memory of a relationship, gives us tremendous strength. It also grants us the adulthood we desperately need. We can forget and then we can remember. You see, when we make peace with our past in our own mind, the strength of our father and mother, and the strength of their father and mother become a wellspring in our own lives.[4]

One of the amazing sagas of recorded history lies in the relationship between Israel and Egypt. With the power of God standing behind her, Israel closed the door on the ghosts of Egypt chasing her. And as her future unfolded, Israel drew strength from an unusual source. In her battle with Assyria, her strongest ally was *Egypt*. In her battle with Babylon, her strongest ally was *Egypt*. When Nebuchadnezzar had sacked the temple and slaughtered its priests, the prophet Jeremiah was rescued by *Egypt*. And in the bleakest days of our recent past as Scud missiles pounded into Tel Aviv from Iraq, Israelis sat huddled in buildings, gas masks on their faces, little children hugging desperately to their mothers' sides, and their only hope the Patriot missiles being off-loaded at ports in *Egypt*.

Consider this Scripture and thought. Matthew 2:13-15 states:

> *When they had gone, an angel of the Lord appeared to Joseph in a dream. "Get up," he said, "take the child and his mother and escape to Egypt. Stay there until I tell you, for Herod is going to search for the child to kill him."*
>
> *So he got up, took the child and his mother during the night and left for Egypt, where he stayed until the death of Herod.*

What a marvelous "new thing" was this miracle as the Holy Family made its way toward Egypt. It totally transformed the circumstances of heritage. Exile became homecoming as the past was scuttled and forgotten. Just as Isaiah had offered assurance, long centuries before, that the people would be redeemed from even their own worst mistakes, so was God once again moving beyond the accumulated wrongful acts in his people's past. Old patterns of reality were breaking up so new realities could begin.

Collectively, socially, and personally the old patterns are there for us: an agrarian heritage; the white, male establishment; a Civil War, still the precursor of much sectionalism; memories of Vietnam. These civilization points converge with individual remembrances of vocational anxiety, the arguments with the spouse and children and the church that at some point was less than it could have been. One of Epiphany's wonders is God's capacity to break up the old patterns of reality and permit us to begin anew. So be it.

---

1. Richard Shenkman, *Legends, Lies, and Myths* (New York: William Morrow and Company, 1988), p. 84.

2. Winona Laduke, "We Are Still Here," *Sojourners* (October, 1991), p. 12.

3. Harold Cooke Phillips, "Closing the Door," in *Sunday Evening Sermons*, edited by Alton M. Motter (New York:Harper), p. 91.

4. *Hazelden Meditations*, June 15, 1986.

Pain And Promise
In The Heart Of God

One of the amazing claims of the Judaeo-Christian heritage is that God takes on the attributes of humans. God's essence is unknown, but the Scriptures claim that God's actions are known. God experiences what humans experience. In the Old Testament God *walks* in the Garden of Eden. God *closes* the door of the ark. God *smells* the fragrance of sacrificed animals. God *chases* Moses in the wilderness.

In like manner Hosea describes God as a wronged husband who seeks to recover his wife who has gone chasing after other lovers. Hosea's own marriage to Gomer is a prophetic symbol of the pain and promise in the heart of God in the face of Israel's faithlessness. Like a brokenhearted husband, God woos back God's bride.

Like an eager and joyous young groom, God had married Israel in the wilderness. The relationship was pure and uncomplicated. Israel had relied solely on her God and God had figuratively made love to Israel in that time of few, if any, competitors for God's affections. But, alas, like a faithless spouse, Israel became a wayward people, leading to the pain of a broken relationship and subsequent divorce.

Hosea begins with a long poem of divorce in which the husband, Yahweh, casts out the fickle spouse. With the image of God as a pained, brokenhearted husband as a backdrop, the lection for today describes Hosea's vision of a resumed marriage between God and God's people. Hosea paints a picture of God's incredible desire to live with this wayward partner.

Perhaps hundreds of sermons are preached each week in our nation on the topic of Hosea and his relationship with Gomer. Unfortunately, the text easily opens itself up to the preacher's whim, allowing the preacher to define as sin whatever in his/her congregation or civilization raises the particular hackles of the moment.

To truly bring this Scripture into a word of God for us today we must cling to history. This word from God through Hosea bears a pain and a promise unlike any other. Hosea is the only prophet who preached to the Northern Kingdom of Israel who was actually born and brought up there. There is no greater pain and promise than preaching to your own people about suffering and hope. To be certain, outside intervention is often necessary to jog a recalcitrant people into action. But it is also less risky and much less intense to deal with other people. We can always tell other people how *they* should respond to *their* children and *their* domestic problems much more easily than we can gain a hearing in our *own* household.

The same is true for the church. The story is told of a preacher in Vermont who was running into some difficulty with his congregation over the strident nature of his sermons. He had lambasted the lack of racial diversity in the town, the high property taxes, the insensitivity of the merchants, and the lack of caring present in family relationships. This was too much, so an ad hoc committee was quickly assembled to meet with the young man to "set him straight." The gathering took place in the church parlor right after worship. The chair began, "Preacher, we are a little worried about the effect your preaching is having on the congregation. When you rail against materialism, the bankers and the merchants find that hard to take. And when you talk against the television preachers pursuing religion for profit, a lot of our folks send money to those people. And when you start talking about family values, why, a lot of our people are busy and commute to Boston and can't just communicate with their children like you envision. And, heck, you make us feel bad about being white and wealthy. Can't you find something else to preach about?"

Totally exasperated, the preacher asked: "Well, what do you people suggest I preach about?"

From the back of the room came a clear voice: "Why don't you preach about the communists?"

"But we don't have any communists in our town, in Vermont," he answered.

"Exactly. Preach about them!"

Hosea has avoided that easy transference. Not only is he speaking to his own people, but his oracles elaborate the theme of the relations between Israel and Yahweh in terms of those between Hosea and his wandering spouse. Hosea's acutely personal experience is used to illumine a conception of a spouse's forgiveness as indicative of Yahweh's ability to reconstitute the entire people of God.

One of the amazing features in the book of Hosea is the notion that words, even The Word, are not enough to turn pain into promise. As Hosea's life unfolds, the prophet's obedience is contrasted with Gomer's disobedience. His faith is shown over and against Gomer's unfaith.

The Old Testament story in all its concrete reality is not removed from our world of harlotry with other gods of wood, stone, and metal, our world of the pursuit of religion for profit, and the political intrigues which consume our national leaders. We must cling to history in order to see specifically that the Old Testament story of Hosea ends at a table surrounded by thirteen men, in an upper room, with one of them holding a cup and saying, "This is the new covenant." The story also ends with some women running from tomb to tomb and telling disbelieving disciples, "He is risen."[1]

Hosea's vision of God as an actor, who in reality turns "not my people" into "my people" again, began to wane in *importance* after his day. After the fall of both kingdoms and the deportation of Judah to Babylon for exile, the majestic qualities of God began to fuel the imaginations of suffering people. Israel began to place her trust in priests who stressed the unapproachable nature of God.

They stressed the holiness of God rather than the activistic, approachable nature of God. They stressed dreams, temples, and angelic visions. In the priestly writings God was spoken of as "holy" or "separate," 161 times! One had to go through a professional priest to experience God, much as one today must use a lawyer to go to court or a pharmacist to secure prescription drugs.

Have you noticed our generation's recent infatuation with angels? If you go to the religion section of major bookstores you'll find that angels are making a big comeback in the world of the unapproachable tele-priests. The spoken word of the sound and stage studio has become the new temple beamed into your living room each day. And satellite religion has enabled us to become farther removed from the point of origin of the word that comes through to us. We take our faith over the cable from people we most likely will never see in person. When we cling to history we see that this is not a new phenomenon. Just as Hosea challenged the remoteness of God from God's people, so did Jesus undo the remoteness of his generation.

After long centuries of having fallen prey to an overemphasis on angelic visions and unapproachable holiness, God's humanity, indeed, God's remarriage to the world was brought back into focus in the life of Christ. The word became flesh, just as it had when Hosea's life served as the vehicle. The God of Jesus Christ walked beside humans, listened to prayers, knew the number of hairs on human heads, welcomed little children to his lap and prodigal children to the kingdom, and even referred to himself as the bridegroom come to remarry the *world*.

These actions of God in Christ, like God in the symbol of Hosea's marriage, are not just for individuals. So often we become duped into thinking of sin as an individual phenomenon. But the Bible, from Hosea through Jesus, doesn't always make a sharp distinction between the individual and society. We tend to sin as a group. We tend to be "not my people" as much as we are "not my person."

Hosea is right. God divorces God's people. We live on an earth where, with all its abundance, over 20 million people die of starvation each year. Over twelve million of those are children under the age of five. In addition to the 30,000 children who starve to death each day are those whom hunger does not kill. Since the brain accomplishes eighty percent of its growth in the first three years of a child's life, no amount of food *later* in life can repair the damage.

What if you were God and your spouse (our world) was doing that to your children? What if your rich spouse, the United States, whom you'd loved in a special way, was spending $24 million an hour on defense? Wouldn't you have a great pain in your heart and want a divorce?

Wouldn't you say "Amen" to that judgment on Golgotha where God says decisively, "You are *not* my people," in light of Jesus Christ illuminating our destructive, rejective ways? Hold to history, then and now, and see the pain in the heart of God.

Ah, but see the utter foolishness and passion of God from Hosea to Christ to the present in the reversal of the prophecies of doom. Yahweh forgives, Christ redeems, not just the individual, but the world God is married to. The people of God are reconstituted. That's the good news of Christ. We have received mercy. The spouse still stands by us and wants us back. We cannot know the promise of Jesus Christ apart from the proclamation of the Old Testament. We cannot know the magnitude of the reconciliation without an awareness of the divorce.

All of us are disobedient, orphaned children, who have rejected our marriage vows to God and are sure to die. And yet — and yet! Like Gomer and ancient Israel and first century Palestine, it is not we who get what we deserve. Christ woos us with love and kindness. Like an eager lover he turns our duty into a joyful affair. All that's asked is that we respond to the promise in the heart of God. So be it!

---

1. See Elizabeth Achtemeier, *The Old Testament and the Proclamation of the Gospel* (Philadelphia: Westminster, 1973), for fuller treatment.

Swing Low,
Sweet Chariot

Many scholars view this narrative as one occasioned by the fear of an uncertain future followed by a sensation of great joy. Indeed, the narrative resolves the transfer of leadership from one generation of prophets to another. There is anxiety over the death of the great Elijah. How will his power be transferred? Who will have the authority when the great man dies?

Certainly the scene is one of crisis. Elisha asks for a "double share" of Elijah's spirit. In Hebrew families the eldest son received a double inheritance. Consequently, Elisha is seeking the firstborn's share of power so he can follow Elijah in the prophetic office. In that day and time a prophet of Israel had to be powerfully equipped to combat the power of the false god, Baal. The scene is one of joy as Elisha has the vision of Elijah's cloak that falls. This passing of Elijah's mantle has often been used in our churches to symbolize the passing of leadership from one person to another.

That a crisis was averted in the death of Elijah is unmistaken. Elijah had exercised tremendous power in behalf of Yahweh (God) in the midst of a dangerous time in Israel. The marriage of Ahab to Jezebel had introduced into Israel the Baal cult which threatened to destroy the very existence of the God of Israel.

The Baal worship was a worship of mere power. And this worship of power became literally the worship of evil. Moral standards fell to an all-time low and the religious life of Israel fell

105

into total disarray. The prophets of Yahweh were killed and most followers were compelled to hide in caves and holes. Consequently, the symbol of Elijah being swept up to the skies in a fiery chariot by a power acting on him from without and Elisha's receiving a double portion of Elijah's spirit meant that enough power was in evidence to fight the false god (Baal) of power.

In many ways the prophet's end was like the man himself. Elijah versus Baal had truly been "fight power with power." "Fight fire with fire." Remember Mount Carmel when Elijah had a fire lighting contest with the prophets of Baal?

It was only fitting that Elijah should be swept up in the skies in tempest and fire. The stormy energy of his career had been symbolized in bloodshed, earthquake, storm, and fire. Certainly nothing could have been more appropriate than a quick lifting to the skies in a fiery, royal chariot in whirlwind and storm.

The Ascension of our Lord Jesus Christ has often been juxtaposed with the Translation of Elijah, to contend that the former is but a "variant" of the latter.[1]

Actually, the epiphany for us may be seen not in similarities but in contrasts. Elijah and Enoch are the only Old Testament personalities taken up into heaven without passing through a human death. God *took* them. They did not ascend. They were carried up.

Like Elijah, Christ's whole life was characterized by the contrasted manner in his end. No blaze of fiery chariot nor agitated tempest was evident to bear Christ heavenward. Christ's whole life had evidenced a power unlike the world recognizes power. his silent gentleness marked him even in his hour of lofty triumph. He moved slowly upward through quiet air. The origin of his ascent was his own will and his own power.

Another striking contrast concerns the transition of authority. Elisha receives a falling mantle, the transference of unfinished business, so he can be fitted for continuing the work which Elijah left undone. An office is passed on so the functions would be the same. That's the way worldly leadership, even religious leadership, tends to operate. Preachers and teachers die and their sons and daughters bow before the new effective preachers and teachers. New arms grasp the mantle to fight fire with fire.

But no one is hailed as Christ's successor. He has left no work unfinished which others may perfect. He has done no work which another may do again. The whole of human nature is taken up to the throne of God in him. His parting is a happy greeting and the portent of an inseparable reunion for us all. It lets us endorse our lives and rise above our miserable time and place. It is the light in our land of shadows.

Perhaps few groups caught the Christ/Elijah contrast more thoroughly than those who sang the old Negro spirituals. They embarked upon these shores called America and to them it was a valley as dark as Jezebel's world in ancient Israel. They were the ultimate victims in a society's worship of power. They stood in the valley of the most serious crisis in American history. The marriage of American society to a system of slavery threatened to destroy the very existence of our civilization. The worship of power over the dignity of human life came from the most hideous immorality imaginable. It was our time to encounter Baal. In their valley of slavery, these victims had not thought of ever having a chance to ride in one of the great chariots or surreys that they saw their bosses riding in. Some cried and died. Some grew angry and festered and boiled inside. Some grabbed the mantle of Elijah and fought fire with fire. Eventually more Americans were killed in that civil war than have been killed in all other wars combined to this very day. Truly the whirlwind and the storm of power descended in greater intensity than ever before. Power battled power.

But still others stood in the fields of North Carolina and Alabama and Mississippi and other places and sang: "Swing low, *sweet* chariot, coming for to carry *me* home."

In that one verse the whole Judaeo-Christian theology was summed up: a new kind of power. The fiery chariot of Elijah, the heavenly pickup from outside, was transformed into a *sweet* chariot.

Perhaps life at times greatly restricts us as to movement, function, and opportunities for leadership. If we live long enough we will no longer have the physical capacity or energy to powerfully affect our own vocational and physical future. Corroding bitterness can enter even the most resilient of hearts, trying to convince us that we are of little significance. We will not be able to fight fire with fire or see the whirlwind. But we can discover that which our Lord insists is the ultimate truth about our destiny. We can validate our spirit as a child of God. Our ability to see the sweetness, to embrace the gentleness, and to look out on the world with quiet eyes will bring forth light into the shadows of our existence. So be it!

---

1. See the excellent work by Alexander Maclaren, *The Secret of Power* (New York: Funk & Wagnalls Company, 1902), pp. 174-186.

Books In This Cycle B Series

Gospel Set
God's Downward Mobility
Sermons For Advent, Christmas And Epiphany
John A. Stroman

Which Way To Jesus?
Sermons For Lent And Easter
Harry N. Huxhold

Water Won't Quench The Fire
Sermons For Pentecost (First Third)
William G. Carter

Fringe, Front And Center
Sermons For Pentecost (Middle Third)
George W. Hoyer

No Box Seats In The Kingdom
Sermons For Pentecost (Last Third)
William G. Carter

First Lesson Set
Light In The Land Of Shadows
Sermons For Advent, Christmas And Epiphany
Harold C. Warlick, Jr.

Times Of Refreshing
Sermons For Lent and Easter
E. Carver McGriff

Lyrics For The Centuries
Sermons For Pentecost (First Third)
Arthur H. Kolsti

No Particular Place To Go
Sermons For Pentecost (Middle Third)
Timothy J. Smith

When Trouble Comes!
Sermons For Pentecost (Last Third)
Zan W. Holmes, Jr.